SHRIMPS, CRAYFISHES, AND CRABS IN THE FRESHWATER AQUARIUM

Uwe Werner

Colorful Longarm-Shrimp, Macrobrachium rosenbergii. *In* Macrobrachium - *species, the second of two pairs of claw-feet is enlarged. (Photo: Sch. Nakano, Archiv A.C.S.)*

Atyopsis moluccensis, *habitus of a beautifully coloured female; Instead of claws, these shrimps have fan-like hands.*

A bright red mangrove-crab, (Sesarma sp.). *The first and only pair of claws-feet is enlarged. (Photo: Sch. Nakano, Archiv A.C.S.)*

Left: Procambarus clarkii *is a north American river crayfish, in which the first of three claw-feet are enlarged.*

Photos by Uwe Werner, if not otherwise mentioned.

We would like to thank the following specialists, companies, breeders and hobbyists for their advice and kindly letting us use their slides:

Schuzo Nakano, Michel Keijman, Frank Teigler, Burkhard Migge, Jens Pinhard, Rüdiger Riehl, W. A. Tomey.

Special thanks to Mary Bailey for her help in many ways.

Aquarium Glaser GmbH,
for providing beautiful fish for our photographers from their weekly imports

amtra - **Aquaristik GmbH,**
for providing furnished aquaria and equipment for testing

Veterinary consultant:
Dr. med. vet. Markus Biffar,
veterinarian, fish specialist

Further useful tips about care and maintenance can be found every six weeks in AQUALOG*news*, the unique newspaper for all friends of the hobby.

Read, for example, the latest breeding reports in the news. It is available in German or English and can be obtained at your local pet shop or subscribed to at the publisher.

Order your free specimen copy!

More information about literature you will find at the end of this book on page 62.

AQUALOG: *Special* - **Serie Ratgeber**
Rodgau: A.C.S.
Shrimps, crayfishes, and crabs in the freshwater aquarium - 2nd edition 2003

English edition: ISBN 3 - 936027 - 08 - 0
German edition: ISBN 3 - 931702 - 99 - 5, 2. neubearb. und erw. Aufl.
(ISBN 3- 931702 - 52 - 9 (first German edtion)

© **Copyright by:**   Verlag A.C.S. GmbH
                        Liebigstr. 1,
                        D-63110 Rodgau
                        Germany

Author:
Uwe Werner
Editor:
Dipl. Biol. Frank Schäfer
Editorial reading of English edition:
Mary Bailey
Cover Layout:
Gabriele Geiß, Büro für Grafik, Frankfurt a.M.

Print, typesetting, processing:
Lithographics: Verlag A.C.S.
Prepress/Photo processing/Layout: Bettina Kirsch
Print: Westermann Druck, Zwickau
Printed on EURO ART,
100 % chlorine free paper

Editors adress:
Verlag A.C.S. GmbH
Liebigstraße 1
D-63110 Rodgau
Fax: +49 (0) 6106 – 64 46 92

E-mail: acs@aqualog.de
http://www.aqualog.de

PRINTED IN GERMANY

Cover Photos:

Front cover
Gercarcinus ruricola – F. Schäfer (a landcrab from Ecuador)
Caridina sp. „serrata", *Procambarus alleni* - Uwe Werner
Back cover
Macrobrachium rosenbergi (S. Nakanao/Archiv A.C.S.), *M.* sp. „luzifugem" (F Schäfer), *Pseudosesarma moeshi, Caridina* "Crystal red" (U. Werner), *Cherax* cf. *papuanus* (F. Schäfer).

Inhalt

Acknowledgements

This book could not have appeared in its current form without the help of Chris Lukhaup, who reviewed the literature and, along with Arne Nolte, provided live American crayfishes, for which my heartfelt thanks. I would also like to thank S. De Grave for identifying a number of shrimps, and Stephan Pflume and Reinhard Pekny for critically reading some sections of the text. Thanks also to Dirk Brandis and Dieter Schaller, who both helped by providing copious encouragement and information. I only regret that it is impossible to include all their ideas within the scope of this book.

Preface

Uwe Werner

Right: River crab of the species Sartoriana spinigera *from India.*

Born in 1948, I have been an aquarist since my childhood, breeding characins and many other fishes, and developing a special interest in the cichlids of Central and South America. My first articles in periodicals and the publication of books followed, and since the beginning of the eighties I have been to the tropics many times to observe fishes in their natural habitats and to bring home a number of species.

My interest in freshwater crustaceans dates back to one of these trips: in 1985, I found some nice freshwater shrimps in Guatemala, took some home, and kept them in my tanks. Later on I found other shrimp and crayfish species, bred

some of them, and reported my experiences in periodicals, and soon was regarded as a specialist - without really being one. It has always been - and still is - a problem to identify the species that are offered for sale in our hobby. This was also true of the first crabs I kept. Trying to find information and help proved to be difficult.

That is why the first edition of this book contained a number of question marks and mistakes which, with the help of various readers, I have now tried to eliminate. But there are still many unanswered questions, and new ones have arisen - in part due to the fact that keeping freshwater crustaceans is becoming more and more popular among aquarists so that the

number of newly imported species is growing rapidly. And so I can only repeat my request to report suggested corrections and additional information to the publisher.

The Australian species Cherax destructor *is, despite it´s mighty claws, a peacefull aquarium inhabitant.*

Systematics
Crayfish and decapods

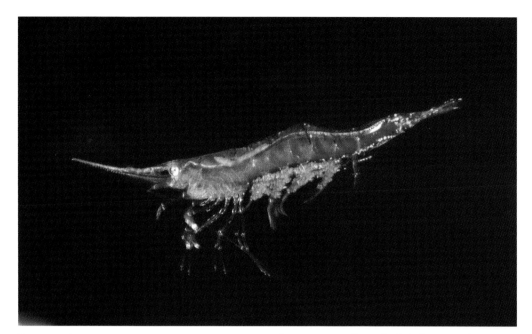

Caridina-*shrimps, here the Red Rhinoceros Shrimp* (Caridina serratirostris) *, have strongly reduced claws, which means that they are completely harmless.*

Systematics

Crayfish and decapods

The class of the crustaceans (Crustacea) consists of a number of different subclasses: for example, the water fleas (*Daphnia*) and copepods such as *Cyclops*, with which the aquarist will be familiar because they are used as fish food, and the fish lice (*Argulus*), which he knows as fish parasites. Apart from these and other lower crustaceans there is the subclass Malacostraca, which contains the so-called higher crustaceans, represented by about 18000 (!) different species, a number corresponding to about half of all known crustaceans. The higher crustaceans are distinguished by their high level of anatomical organisation, their astonishing variety of forms, and the wide range of different natural habitats they have conquered. Other reasons include their highly developed behaviour and - last but not least - their size. The so-called decapods (Decapoda) in this group are the largest living arthropods. There are giant Antarctic shrimp species with a length of 60 centimetres, giant Australian crayfish with thorny armour, Indo-Australian (marine) crabs with a carapace 40 centimetres wide, and giant Japanese spider crabsliving in the deep sea, whose walking legs span about three metres.

The order Decapoda is divided into two suborders: the Natantia (swimming crustaceans) and the Reptantia (walking/creeping crustaceans). To the Natantia belong all shrimp-like forms, normally called shrimps and prawns: crustaceans with a body deeper than wide and a thin shell, which are good swimmers, able to swim forwards using their pleopods. They have two pairs of claws, which in *Macrobrachium* species are enlarged to a different degree: the smaller, anterior claws are used for eating, and the larger, second pair for threatening and fighting. The Natantia include - *inter alia* - the freshwater shrimps of the families Atyidae and Palaemonidae. The Reptantia include all the forms that primarily walk rather than swim and have a thick shell. They are divided into four groups:

1) The Astacidea, the lobster- or crayfish-like crustaceans, include, *inter alia*, the marine lobster family (Homaridae) and the true river crayfishes, usually called simply crayfishes. These have three pairs of claws, the first pair of which are enlarged. Their body is less deep than wide and they walk forwards, but swim (using their pleon) only backwards. They are referred to three families: the Old World river crayfishes (Astacidae), the New World river crayfishes (Cambaridae) - both of which are represented by many genera and species in the northern hemisphere (northern hemisphere river crayfishes) - and the Parastacidae, which live in the southern hemisphere (southern hemisphere river crayfishes). The latter are distributed in southern South America, New Zealand, Australia/New Guinea, and Madagascar. The Australian crayfishes are often regarded as a separate family, the Austroastacidae

2. The Palinura or spiny lobsters comprise only marine species and have large, clawed antennae rather than large claws. Most species are very tasty, but cannot be kept in freshwater aquaria.

3. The Anomura are crays with a large asymmetrical tail; they are a large group rich in forms, and some species are rather interesting for the freshwater aquarist. These include the Aeglidae from South America: elongated crustaceans, reminiscent of the river crayfishes, which live in the rivers and lakes of subtropical South America. During the breeding period the females of some species leave the water and congregate under stones or dead wood. From their eggs emerge completely developed young. The Paguridae (the hermit crabs), which protect their abdomens in spiral shells, include a number of terrestrial species that can be kept in terraria without difficulty (*Coenobita*).

4. The Brachyura (the true crabs) have their abdomen folded beneath the greatly broadened anterior part of the body. They have only one pair of claws - which are greatly enlarged. They include the true freshwater crabs (Potamoidea), the mangrove crabs (Grapsidae), the running crabs and fiddler crabs (Ocypodidae), and the true land crabs (Gecarcinidae).

Drawing: Crayfish after
MERRIK & LAMBERT (1991)

The decapods, their exo- and endo-skeleton

The morphology and anatomy of crustaceans makes them interesting subjects for study. The body consists of two main parts: the immovable cephalothorax (united head and thorax), which is rather long in shrimps and crayfishes but short and wide in crabs (Brachyura); and the pleon or abdomen, which can be moved backwards and forwards and ends in the telson, which in most cases is triangular, and beneath which we find the anus.

At first glance you will notice the pair of strongly-developed "arms" with claws, which are termed chelipeds (= "claw-feet"). Behind these follow four pairs of legs which serve for walking, and are called peraeopods (= "walking legs"). The chelipeds are, essentially, specialised walking-legs. Their penultimate segment forms a stiff finger-like element, against which closes a movable "finger". The chelipeds and legs each consist of seven segments (sometimes two of them are fused, such that only six can be counted). If you add the two chelipeds to the thoracic limbs, then you have a total of ten „feet", which explains the name Decapoda (= „ten-footers") given to the order. In front of the peraeopods we find the mouthparts, consisting of a pair of mandibles, two pairs of maxillae, and three pairs of maxillipeds (= "jaw-feet"), the posteriormost of which are of considerable size.

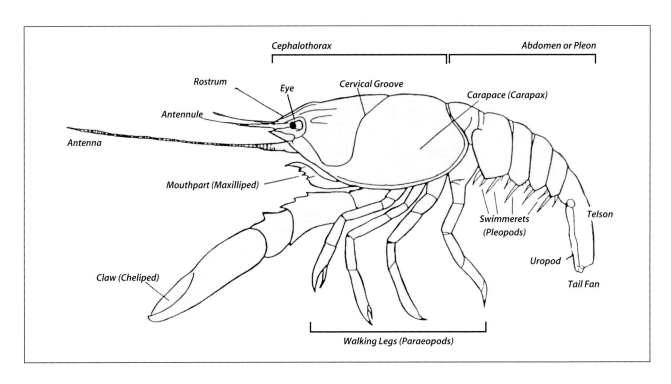

Morphology, anatomy, biology
The decapods, their exo- and endo-skeleton

Empty shell of a longarm-shrimp.

The maxillipeds bear lateral appendages, which in part move the water for respiration and in part serve as gills.

On the abdomen we find limbs with a completely different structure, usually five pairs of so-called abdominal legs or pleopods. These exhibit the original fissiped structure and are used for swimming, producing a current of water, and reproduction. They consist of a basal segment, on which are located two branches, one exterior and one interior (exopoid and endopoid). Originally all the limbs were built like this, but some have been modified for walking and feeding. Today the walking legs (peraeopods) consist almost entirely of the inner branch, while the outer has been reduced. On the basal part of the peraeopods there are multiple appendages that form gills. The mandibles and (in long-tailed forms) the last pleopods are highly specialised, the latter, together with the telson, forming the tail fan, and thus termed uropods (= "tail feet"). If a crayfish jerks its abdomen to and fro, the tail fan causes a sudden backward impetus, which crays often use to flee. In male river crayfishes and crabs the first two pairs of pleopods are modified for reproduction, forming tube-like copulatory organs that transmit the sperm. In addition, females carry the fertilised eggs and embryos around on their pleopods.

The body of the crustacean is covered by a hard skin (the cuticula), which is composed in part of calcium carbonate and thus forms a solid shell. The anterior part of the body and the gills, which are located on the sides, are covered by a shield -like structure, the carapace, which forms two respiratory or gill chambers, one on each sides. It serves as an exterior skeleton (exo-skeleton), protecting the body tissue and the gills inside. In terrestrial forms the "ceiling" of the gill chamber contains finely ramified blood vessels and serves as a kind of lung, enabling the animal to breathe air. Crustaceans with a lung of this type will suffocate in water that is low in oxygen if there is no possibility to take up air.

In addition the muscles are attached to the inner surface of this armour. To this end, at least in larger crustaceans, excrescences are present on the inner surface such that the exterior skeleton is continued in places by an inner one (the endoskeleton). This is especially important for the gizzard, which is situated in the anterior part of the body and whose numerous muscles require firm attachment points. The cervical groove on the carapace represents the posterior edge of the head. In crabs, a system of such grooves indicates the positions of certain organs. In some crustaceans the shell may itself be a multi-angled construction. The anterior part of the carapace is pointed, forming a more or less protruding rostrum. This corresponds to the forehead in crabs, and is flanked by "cut-outs" for the eyes, from which the movable eye-stalks with their bulging eyes protrude.

Preserved crabs of the genus Demanietta *with lifted pleon, so that the sexual organs can be seen.*

female

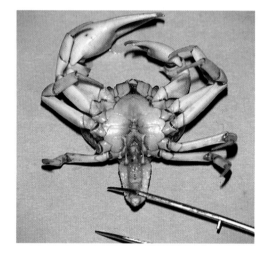

male

less "buttercrayfish" gets to its feet with difficulty, searching for shelter. It will hide for the next two or three days, until the new carapace has hardened.

This happens through the hardening of chitin and the absorption of calcium carbonate. The claws stiffen first, then the rest of the shell. Most of the necessary calcium carbonate is taken from the water via the gills, but a small amount is collected before the moult and secreted or stored in paired gastroliths in the stomach (or proventiculus). Initially the gastroliths are small and plate-like, but as further calcium carbonate is deposited, they assume the shape of a button. The empty shell is, by the way, almost never left to decompose, but usually eaten within a few days by the newly-moulted crustacean (or any other finding it), which permits the further recycling of mineral salts.

Crustaceans grow for as long as they live, but more slowly with age, which means that moulting occurs with decreasing frequency. Young crustaceans may moult within a few days or even hours after hatching, young adult crustaceans moult four or five times a year, old individuals only once or twice a year. The glands that induce and control the moults and the production of chitin are, by the way, situated in the eye-stalks of the "ten-footers".

The coloration of crustaceans is composed of pigments which are embedded in the shell. Most of them are reddish, brownish, or bluish. But crustaceans are also able to change their colours: this happens (as in fish) in two different ways, gradually (controlled by hormones) or in a flash (controlled by the nervous system) by the expansion or contraction of colour cells (chromatophores) in the underlying skin tissue. The coloration of smaller crustaceans may be partially due to coloured (red or yellow) fat-balls inside the body or by the (green or blue) content of the gut. The crabs, which also adjust their own coloration to that of their surroundings, control it using eye-stalk hormones.

When crustaceans die, the albuminous pigment of the shell (Astaxanthin) can break down more or less completely and at variable speed into its albumen and pigments (carotinoid) components, so that the shell assumes an intense orange or red coloration. This happens most rapidly and intensely under the influence

Growth and coloration

Because of their rigid carapace, crustaceans do not grow gradually, but in a series of steps related to moults. Each such step is signalled by the fact that they stop eating. Stimulated by a hormone, the crustacean leaves its old shell within a few minutes, jerking and wrenching heavily. Shrimps and crayfishes emerge from the old shell through a split in the neck. In crabs it is the back edge of the carapace that bursts open, and they lift the dorsal shell like the lid of a box, sliding out backwards.

The new shell, wrinkly and too large, then fills with water and tightens. And then, while they are still soft and lethargic, the crustaceans grow, replacing limbs formerly lost, completely or at least to a certain degree (smaller in size). After the moult they lie about apathetically for some time, noticeably lighter-coloured than before. Eventually the often soft and defence-

Morphology, anatomy, biology
Sex discrimination and reproduction

Female Caridina-*sprimp ("Bee-Shrimp") with rather big eggs, an example for the more specialized mode of reproduction.*

of heat, for example if they are dropped in boiling water.

Sex discrimination and reproduction

In many cases it is not easy to determine the sex of shrimps reliably, but females usually have a broader pleon and the sides of the pleon segments extend further downward. In some groups the size and colour of the claws is different, and among the Atyids the males have special appendages on their legs, for holding females. The pleopods are not very specialised, and although males do have a so-called appendix masculinus (male appendage) on the first pair of pleopods, this is barely visible in live specimens. Copulation often takes place quickly and mostly at night.

In river crayfishes the sperm packets are usually deposited on the ventral surface of the female and the eggs are fertilised externally after they emerge. These crayfishes also copulate belly to belly. Females of some related groups have a special opening (the annulus ventralis) or indentation (thelycium)

Female Chocó-shrimp, belonging to the Macrobrachium- *or longarm-shrimps, with tiny eggs, an example for te primitive mode of reproduction.*

on their underside, into which sperm packets can be deposited and stored for some time.

The sex of crabs is easy to determine by the shape and width of the abdomen: in females the pleon is very wide, oval, and occupies a large part of the posterior body, while in males it is narrow and triangular. The genital openings are sometimes situated at the base of the third pair of legs in females, but further back in males, at the base of the fifth pair. In many crabs the genital openings of females are to be found on the third segment of the sternum.

The pleopods of male crabs and river crayfishes form the gonopods, by means of which the sperm packets are transferred onto or into the genital openings of females. Essentially, in male crabs all the other pairs of pleopods are atrophied. In females numerous pairs of pleopods are developed and covered with copious bristles. They also have glands which are used to attach the eggs to the pleopods - they carry the fertilised eggs and even the newly-hatched larvae or young around on their pleopods.

During copulation in crabs, the tips of the anterior gonopods are inserted into the female genital openings. To this end, both partners bend their pleon down and the female is usually turned onto her back. After the gonopods have been inserted, sperm masses are pumped into the female's genital openings. This may take some hours during which the crabs seem to be totally immune to disturbance. Many marine species are able to copulate only when the female has recently moulted and her shell is soft, as, once the shell has hardened, a kind of chalky grating blocks the genital opening. In crabs the eggs are fertilised in the genital ducts of the females.

Modes of reproduction

When it comes to the development of their eggs, decapods practise two completely different methods of reproduction. The first, the "specialised method", sometimes known as direct development, is found in all river crayfishes and in some shrimps and crabs: the young become almost fully-formed inside the eggs, which are especially large and yolk-rich,

and, after hatching from the eggshell, resemble their parents in all respects and need only to develop their sexual organs; they eat more or less the same food as adults, and, last but not least, are relatively large right from the start and grow fast, so that they have a good chance of surviving their first days of independent life. For all these reasons it is quite easy to breed these decapods under aquarium conditions. The eggs are not very numerous (their number depends on the size and condition of the female and may be up to 300) but rather large. The young and omnivorous crayfishes are tended by their mother, feeding voraciously and growing rapidly.

The second, more basic or primitive type of reproduction, is known as indirect development. This mode of reproduction is found in marine decapods and species that lay their eggs in brackish or salt water, as is the case in many shrimps and crabs. The eggs develop into tiny larvae which have only few body segments and limbs. The most simple larval form is called the nauplius, which has three pairs of limbs and is hardly ever seen in decapods. Almost all decapods instead start life as zoea larvae which look like primitive shrimps. In the course of a number of moults they develop a greater number of body segments and limbs and change into fully-formed crustaceans. All the larval stages usually have highly specialised environmental requirements that may vary at each successive developmental stage. They often travel enormous distances across a variety of marine regions, before returning as juveniles to rivers or coastal regions. Hence it is almost impossible to rear them under aquarium conditions. And Nature allows for considerable losses: females of some species that practice this primitive method of reproduction produce several hundred thousand (!) eggs.

Sensory organs

The eyes of decapods are mostly, but not always, located on eye stalks, and are complex or faceted – this can even be seen in photos of zoea larvae taken with an electron microscope - and very efficient. In crabs in particular they are highly developed: in some species there are up to thirty thousand single eyes (ommatids) on each eye-stalk, while in others there are "only" seven thousand facets. The poorest sight is found in some crayfish

Morphology, anatomy, biology
Modes of reproduction, sensory organs

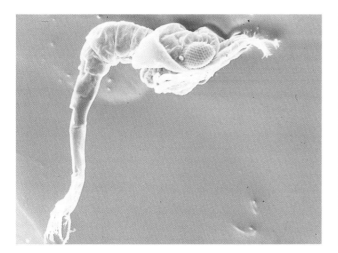
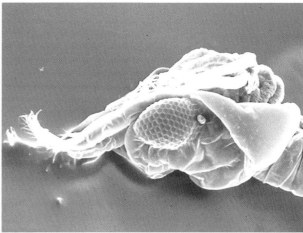

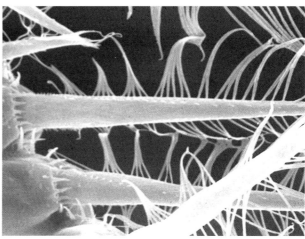

larvae, which depend on a mere twenty sight cells. Crustaceans from deep waters or cave-dwelling species may have atrophied eyes. In such cases the animals orientate principally by their senses of touch and smell..

Crustaceans are able to detect not only different degrees of brightness, but also shapes and colours. Not for nothing are many species so colourful, and their claws strikingly large or intensely coloured. Their range of sight should also be mentioned - it comprises 360 degrees, so they can rely on complete all-round vision. Besides which, they can also detect stationary objects. These abilities give rise to others: some crustaceans, above all certain crabs, are able to find their way using the travel and position of the sun and perhaps also the moon, so that they can undertake long migrations. They can also detect potential dangers from a long way away: a person, for example, can be spotted from a distance of about 19 metres, so that the crab

has enough time to make its escape.

On the head there are two small and one large pairs of antennae. In shrimps and crayfishes these are particularly conspicuous, growing to about as long as the body, whereas in most crabs they are weakly developed. In addition, in crabs the first pair of antennae can be folded and concealed in special grooves beneath the rostrum, so that they can barely be seen. The first or basal segment of each of the first (smaller) antennae contains an organ of balance (statocyst). This consists of a kind of small skin bag which is filled with water from outside and in which are embedded so-called statoliths, which are either manufactured by the crustacean or taken in from outside. In most cases crayfishes use grains of sand. When they moult, they lose these as well as the shell, and have to make or take in new ones. The function of these little stones can be easily explained: as the crustacean leans in any direction, they press against

Zoea-larvae of a Macrobrachium *species, photographed with an elecronic microscope, showing the habitus (the legs are directed forward), the head with the facet-eye, the tail-fan and details of the tail-fan. (Photo: R. Riehl)*

Upper left: Mouth of an unidentified crab (Photo: Migge / Archiv A.C.S.)

Upper right: The picture of this Fiddler-crab beautifully shows the facet-eyes on the eye-stalks. (Photo: Nakano / Archiv A.C.S.)

M. left: This Macrobrachium *from Guatemala is turning a food tablet in its brushy hands to feed on the tiny particles.*

Middle right: This Atya gabonensis *is catching plankton, spreading its fan-like hands.*

Large picture: This Cardisoma armatum *feeds on a frozen female fish. The claws are passing the food to the mandibles.*

Morphology, anatomy, biology
Respiration, blood circulation, digestion

sensory hairs, indicating its orientation to the animal. Crustaceans can also detect rotation by virtue of the inertial mass of the statoliths.

The larger or "second" antennae are the most important organs of touch. They are extremely mobile and can be directed not only forwards and to both sides, but also completely backwards. They are used for orientation and enable the crustacean to move safely at any time of day (day, night) and in any environmentally-dictated half-light (in caves, under stones). In addition, fine sensory hairs on the mouthparts, claws, legs, and abdomen provide exceptional sensitivity to the slightest tactile stimuli.

The senses of smell and taste depend on numerous tubular cells (aesthetasks) that are located on the first antennae and which are sensitive to substances dissolved in water, and perhaps also to air-borne smells. Further organs of taste are to be found on the ends of the legs, and, of course, on the mouthparts.

Respiration, blood circulation, digestion

Most crustaceans breathe by means of gills. In shrimps and crayfishes these are clustered or tufted (trichobranchia), consisting of a shaft from which extend numerous small cylindrical appendages. The gills of crabs consist of double rows of close-packed plates (phyllobranchia). The water needed for gas exchange flows in through a number of ventrally-located openings between the edge of the carapace and the leg insertions, flowing out again via forward-opening gill slits in shrimps and crayfishes, while crabs have a wide outlet near the mouth. Gas exchange takes place via the fine gill membranes. The gill lamellae contain haemolymph which carries oxygen to the organs and gives off CO_2.

The heart is whitish in live individuals and is located in front of the posterior edge of the cephalothorax, contained in a kind of bag, the pericardium. There are no veins, just four slit-like openings that act like valves, opening and closing as the heart expands and contracts. Two large arteries run from the heart, one forwards to the head, the other backwards to supply the pleon. Both are open-ended and the blood is then further distributed via interstices in the tissues until it is eventually sucked back in by the heart (open circulation).

The food is in most cases seized by the claws and passed to the mouthparts. The maxillipeds hold the food, and pieces are then cut off by the strong hard mandibles, sometimes with the aid of other mouthparts. Via the mouth opening these pieces reach the anterior part of the gut, which consists largely of a gigantic gizzard. This contains numerous variably-shaped chitinous teeth that chop up the food and mix it with digestive enzymes. In the rear part of the gizzard complex filter systems remove indigestible components and transport them to the mid-gut, from where they are excreted. The digestible material is transported into lateral sac-like appendages behind the gizzard, the central gut glands, which extend throughout the anterior body and function much like our liver. Here the actual digestion and uptake of substances takes place.

The end-products of metabolism are excreted via nephritic ducts which end near the second antennae, i.e. on the head (!). Most of these excreta are urinary compounds such as ammonia or ammonium salts, etc. These substances are also in part excreted via the gills.

The most well-known Caridina-shrimp is this species, mostly referred to as Caridina *"serrata" - here a male.*

Shrimps
Atyids: *Caridina*-species

Shrimps

Atyids: *Caridina*-shrimps

In the sub-order of long-tailed shrimp-like crustaceans (Natantia) we find two families which are highly interesting for the aquarist, i.e. the freshwater shrimps (Atyidae) and - from the super-family Palaemonoidea - the Palaemonidae, to which belong the shrimps of the Baltic Sea and the *Macrobrachium* species.

The Atyids represent an, evolutionarily-speaking, very old family of shrimps and include mostly freshwater species. A number of them are found in Asia and Africa, the others in South America. They have been classified in 15 different genera containing about 160 species. Typical features of some atyids include, according to E. &. U. LEIENDECKER (1982), "a brush-like pilosity of both pairs of claw-bearing legs and a tendency to reduction of the rostrum, expressed to a greater or lesser extent depending on the genus concerned". In other words, the delicate claws of these shrimps have been transformed into heavily bristled "hands", and the pointed "nose" is often short. In other Atyids, here termed the *Caridina* group, the claws are no more than tiny

The species in question belong to the genera *Caridina* and *Neocaridina* - which the aquarist who is not a biologist will certainly not be able to distinguish - and grow to a size of between two and four centimetres. They are distributed in Africa, tropical and sub-tropical Asia, and the islands of the western Pacific. As far as number of species is concerned, the genus *Caridina* is one of the largest in the family, with more than 120 species. Unfortunately it is almost impossible to identify the individual species, and so in the following text I have used popular names that have become more or less generally accepted.

These *Caridina* and the closely related *Neocaridina* are completely harmless, quite unable to inflict any damage with their tiny claws. Instead we need to protect them from attack by larger fishes which might take them for a tasty snack. If you want to keep them in a community tank, it should contain only small, peaceful fishes. It is, however, better to keep these shrimps with their own kind - a small aquarium with a capacity of about 10 litres will suffice. Provide a lot of fine-leaved plants and plenty of light, so that algae will grow abundantly, and you will satisfy their most important needs. Avoid keeping the tank too clean because these animals feed on all types of algae, plant debris, and other organic waste, e.g. dead aquatic animals. Even so they should periodically be given fine flake food or food tablets. They do best only when a layer of mulm has developed – for this reason it is best not to include a filter, just a stream of fine airbubbles.

And don't forget that in the natural habitat all these *Caridina* shrimps live together in densely-populated colonies, so you shouldn't keep just one or two of them, but a proper group.

Most species thrive not only at high temperatures (up to 28°C), but also in cooler water (18 to 21°C), but basically it is better to keep them within a temperature range of 23 to 25°C in the long term, rather than too warm. Soft water doesn't seem to be an unconditional requirement condition for keeping them successfully, but is preferable to hard water (above 10°dGH). At the same time, the pH should be below neutral. Always remember that these shrimps react badly to the slightest trace of copper, so water that has stood for a long time in copper pipes should be avoided, as should medications containing copper.

Most of the *Caridina* species that are offered for aquarium maintenance practice the specialised mode of reproduction - which means that they produce relatively large eggs from which hatch fully-formed young shrimps. Females, which have a special brood chamber for their eggs on the abdomen, can be recognised by their stockier, deeper body, while males are more slender and have longer swimmerets.

The eggs are large, ranging from 20 to 30 in number, and can be seen through the carapace when the light is from behind. They develop over a period of 28 to 33 days, eventually hatching into not larvae but well-developed young shrimps that have already gone through all the larval stages in the egg, so that it is easy to raise them. Moreover they don't need any special feeding if they are kept in an "old", well-planted aquarium with a lot of algae. In addition, the adults do not eat their

Shrimps
Atyids: *Caridina*-species

Left: Caridina *sp. I, the "Back-stripe Shrimp", is not very colourful.*

Right: Caridina *sp. II, the "Spotted Shrimp", is characterized by black spots on the back and on the abdomen.*

Left: Caridina *sp. IV, the "Bumblebee Shrimp", shows broad orange or brown vertical bands. A picture of the "Bee Shrimp".* Caridina *sp. III can be found on page 11.*

Right: Caridina *sp. V, the "Tiger Shrimp", shows a characteristic pattern of dark-brown stripes.*

Large picture: This is the so-called "Crystal Red", a colour-form of the "Bee-Shrimp".

young. The latter attain sexual maturity within 3 to 6 months.

The best-known shrimp in the *Caridina* group is an attractively coloured "zebra shrimp" which is generally known as *Caridina serrata*. It is imported from Hongkong - as are a number of other freshwater shrimps – and hence the species may perhaps be *C. cantonensis*. According to a recent revision of the genus there is, in fact, a so-called "*serrata*-group" of closely related, morphologically similar, species, which includes *C. cantonensis*, *C. sphyrapoda*, *C. nanoensis*, *C. apodosis*, *C. yulinica*, *C. wumingensis*, and *C. mutata*, as well as *C. serrata*. Nearly all of them are known from limited distributions, live mainly in running water and avoid brackish water. The water is supposedly rather soft and slightly acid (pH 6.8).

Occasionally other small shrimps of this group are imported, probably *Caridina* species, although their actual identity is unknown. *Caridina* sp. I, the Back-stripe Shrimp, supposedly grows no larger than four centimetres. It differs from *C. serrata* by having a shorter rostrum and

Female of Caridina *"serrata" with some eggs shining through the body.*

a stouter body - the cephalothorax and the abdomen are more powerfully built, so that the animals look rather stocky - and in its coloration: a more or less prominent (according to mood) light longitudinal band extends along the brownish back from the rostrum to the start of the telson.

Caridina sp. II, the Spotted Shrimp, does not grow as big as *C. serrata* and is orange-brown, but not intensely coloured. The rear parts of the body in particular are adorned with irregularly distributed black spots.

Caridina sp. III, the Bee Shrimp, is a sturdily built

little shrimp with a short rostrum. Its tail fan is tinged with orange, and there are whitish bands or blotches on the posterior part of the brown back. Isolated white spots are also found on the head, specifically behind the eye and on the neck region, while the rest of the cephalothorax is more or less uniform brown.

Caridina sp. IV, the Bumblebee Shrimp, is similar to the last-mentioned species, but has no white markings. There are three broad, clearly defined, bands on the body, the first of which sometimes merges dorsally with a large spot in the eye region. These bands are reddish-brown or dark brown, and the spaces between them light and transparent.

Caridina sp. V, the Tiger Shrimp, is more elongate than all the other species mentioned and is easily recognisable by its yellowish-transparent body adorned with narrow but prominent brown diagonal stripes, especially on its posterior part. It too has an orange-tinged tail fan.

There are also bright red and white, so-called Crystal Red shrimps that have been created in Japan from mutations of both the Bee Shrimp and Zebra Shrimp, which explains why there are both stocky and elongate Crystal Reds. such forms are rarely if ever found in nature and their offspring are not all the same colour. If you want to maintain the intense coloration, you will have to select only the most beautiful for breeding!

The Amano Shrimp, *Caridina japonica*, is also known as the Algae Shrimp, the Yamamoto Shrimp, and the Japanese Shrimp. Even though it is not very colourful, it has become quite popular because it is an algae-eater *par excellence*. It eats even tough and firmly attached algae, and also feeds on plant detritus. It is imported from Japan and has a transparent or milky body. Its body is adorned with small brownish spots arranged in rows. Females are deeper-bodied and larger - they grow to about six centimetres - and are easily recognised by the distinctive brood chamber on the abdomen.

These shrimps are very tolerant as regards water temperature (which may range from 15 to 28°C), hardness, and pH, but, unlike the species discussed earlier, they prefer hard alkaline water. Use of medications always

Shrimps
Atyids: *Caridina*-species

poses a risk. If conditions are to their liking they often swim in the open water.

The Amano Shrimp practices the primitive mode of reproduction. The incubation time for its up to 2000 eggs is about six weeks at a temperature range of 23 to 27°C and a pH of between 5.8 and 8.0. Unfortunately it produces not tiny shrimps but larvae that measure no more than 1 to 1.5 mm and are of a milky transparency. These have to be transferred to brackish water with a salt content of 1.6 % and must be fed the tiniest foods (Liquifry, Micromin, Protogen-Granulat or the like). In the course of four weeks and several moults and stages, the larvae develop into young shrimps that have to be acclimated slowly to fresh water.

Another closely related *Caridina* species is imported which is similar in coloration but lacks spots. This species, here termed *Caridina* sp. cf. *japonica*, also produces numerous small, greenish-grey eggs. This is also true of another species which is sold as *Caridina serratirostris* or the Red Rhinoceros Shrimp. It is not yet known if these small shrimps can be bred in the same way and under similar conditions to *C. japonica*.

Atyids are also found in the European region: *Atyaephyra desmaresti* is a small shrimp that was originally found in fresh and brackish waters in southern Europe and northern Africa, but in 1909 appeared for the first time in the Dortmund-Ems Canal and has since then shown up in the in the Rhine, the Mittelland Canal, the rivers Leine (near Hannover), Havel (near Berlin), and Lippe (and in the Lippe Canal). It has even been reported from the Netherlands and Belgium. Its preference for canals has led to its being commonly referred to as Canal Shrimp. The species is usually translucent, but brown or blue shades are possible and it is able to change its colour just as other species do. Females of this "minishrimp" grow to 35 mm long, a good centimetre longer than males. The species seems to live no longer than a year and a half and should be kept in cold water, even though it tolerates temperatures up to 25°C for a short time. They will eat algae and small aquatic organisms, and also flake food. In the wild, females carry up to 1500 eggs from the beginning of April until the end of August. Juveniles of about 6 mm can be

found from June onwards, and attain about two centimetres by the end of the year.

The Amano Shrimp - here a female - can be recognized by its characteristic spots and lines.

This Caridina *sp. cf.* japonica *(upper picture a female, lower a male) lacks these spots.*

Below: Atyaephyra desmaresti *has become known as the "Canal Shrimp".*

Atyids: Fan shrimps

Atyids: Fan shrimps

The Atyid family is named after the shrimp genus *Atya*, which it includes. In the aquarium hobby they are known from the fan shrimps, but there are also species no fans, and some where only some individuals have fan hands.

The genera

Atyopsis (with two species between Singapore, the Philippines, and New Zealand) and *Atya* (12 species in South and Central America as well as tropical West Africa) are of aquarium importance. In particular, *Atyopsis moluccensis* is regularly imported, and perhaps also the similarly coloured *A. spinipes*. *A. moluccensis* has seven to sixteen serrate teeth on the rostrum, whereas *A. spinipes* has only two to six rather larger teeth on a less pointed rostrum.

As far as is known, *A. moluccensis* is found not only on the Moluccas, but also on many southeast Asian islands and also on the mainland continent. But it is still unclear whether the differently coloured, anatomically identical, forms represent mere colour variants and local forms, or are valid species. Female *A. moluccensis* grow to at least six, males to about eight, centimetres, or even more.

Atyopsis moluccensis is in great demand on account of its coloration, but it is not so much the colour itself as the ability to change colour that is the attraction. Young specimens always have a light dorsal band running from the rostrum to the beautiful fan-like tail. Despite reports to the contrary, this band does not disappear in older specimens, though it may become less prominent in time. In addition these shrimps can change their colour in seconds, apparently randomly, but perhaps depending on mood or in response to light levels or their surroundings. Sometimes they are marbled yellowish-brown, more often intense dark brown and sometimes even brown-red or red. Perhaps some observant aquarist who keeps records will be able to make some kind of sense of this chamaeleon-like behaviour......

In the meantime, a second *Atyopsis* species has become available. It is imported from Asia, grows a little larger than *A. moluccensis* and looks rather similar, but its ground colour is more brownish and the stripe on the back is always beige rather than golden.

It must be said that these shrimps are not really elegant animals. The general impression is, on the contrary, that the high heavy shell is quite a burden, and follows the slow movements of the legs only with difficulty and in jerks. That they seem to be clumsy animals is also due to the short rostrum, which is significantly shorter than that of the Palaemonids (which will be discussed later), and that the head and the body are not separate, but, so to speak, "melded" into one another. The impression that there is not much life in these animals is reinforced by the small eyes, which are located close to the head and not on long eye-stalks as in other shrimps.

This impression is reinforced by the short legs, three pairs of which are sited rather far forward, so that the rear part of the body seems to be dragged along behind. Nevertheless these shrimps climb with great agility, at least under water. Sometimes you will find them, clinging to a few strands of algae, on the vertical panes of the tank, or are hanging, back downwards, on a floating plant leaf, with no obvious clues as to how they got there. Hence you should never underestimate their climbing abilities and bear in mind that they may clamber out of the tank!

Atya and *Atyopsis* can easily be differentiated from other genera because their claws have been transformed into strange brush-like "hands". Fine bristles are to be found on both "fingers" of the claw, forming a sort of semi-circular fan, the two "fingers" creating a completely circular "trap" that can be opened wide, but also folded closed.

Under aquarium conditions you will be able to observe how the shrimps open their hands to catch food items, holding the latter as if in a closed hand and then conveying them to their mouths.

We can deduce from this that *Atya* and *Atyopsis* live in running, or at least moving, water where they do not actually "search" for food, but position themselves in a suitable,

Shrimps
Atyids: Fan shrimps

Left: The males of Atyopsis moluccensis grow to a bigger size than the females - here a pair.

This A. moluccensis is searching for food at the ground, using its fan-like hands.

Atya gabonensis can be pink to rosy, but also bluish-grey.

Shrimps
Atyids: Fan shrimps

Left: In males of the fan shrimps - here Atyopsis moluccensis - *it is the first pair of walking-legs that is bigger.*

Right: This Atya *sp. was caught in southern Mexico in a Grijalva-tributary.*
(Photo: M. Keijman)

Left: This brown Atya *is imported from Brazil and is sold as "Brown Giant Fanshrimp".*
(Photo: F. Teigler / Archiv A.C.S.)

Right: In the mountain rivers of Honduras (Atlantic slope) we found these Atya *, which are also bred on farms.*

elevated, position, spreading their fan-hands like parabolic antennae in front of and above themselves in order to catch particles of plankton.

In the aquarium, of course, you will be able to observe this behaviour only if the filter produces a suitably strong current. Otherwise the shrimps will search for food on the bottom, covering any edible material with their hands and grasping it. They seldom take larger morsels, so it is best to feed *Artemia* nauplii, pond plankton, and fine flake food. They eagerly feed on food tablets that slowly disintegrate into tiny pieces when put in water.

Recently fan shrimps of the genus *Atya* have also been imported from West Africa. The distribution of this genus encompasses not only parts of Africa (the Atlantic side from Senegal to northern Angola), but also large areas of Central and South America (Pacific slope from northern Mexico to Peru; Atlantic side from Mexico down to southern Brazil).

Astonishingly the species most commonly offered for sale, *Atya gabonensis*, occurs in both West Africa and eastern South America. This shrimp grows to a total length of about 15 centimetres and is usually sold as the Cameroon Shrimp, Blue Fan Shrimp, or Giant African Freshwater Shrimp.

These shrimps too are strikingly attractive and can change their colour in the same way as *A. moluccensis*. Most of the time they are bluish-grey or brownish, sometimes even yellowish, with a pink tinge. The cephalothorax and the abdomen are smooth, but the legs are covered with dark "warts", which are particularly well developed in males. These shrimps are particularly light-coloured (pink or flesh-coloured) after moulting. They are apparently also able to change their colour depending on their mood, light levels, and the colour of their surroundings. As in *A. moluccensis*, females remain significantly smaller than males.

In the Caribbean region Atyids (*Micratya poei; Atya innocous*) are distributed both on the mainland and on the islands.

Unfortunately they have not yet featured in aquarium magazines. I myself found a

Shrimps
Atyids: Fan shrimps

Left: Atya gabonensis - here a beige coloured individual - taking up food from the ground.

Right: Atyopsis moluccensis, here a female with an intensely golden strimpe along its back.

Left: This Atyopsis has been imported from Asia: it resembles A. moluccensis, but grows to a bigger size.

Right: Sitting on a piece of wood, this decently coloured Atyopsis-species can rarely be seen.

brownish-marbled shrimp of this type in a number of rivers on the Atlantic side of Honduras, another in Lake Catemaco in southern Mexico, a third in the southern highlands of Chiapas in tributaries of the Grijalva River, and I have seen photos of a similar *Atya* species from Brazil.

There are so far no reports in the aquarium literature concerning the completely successful breeding of the Asian and African *Atyopsis* or *Atya*. What we do know is that males develop a much stronger first pair of walking legs, the third segment of which becomes particularly thick.

GÖTHEL (1986) observed that females of *A. moluccensis* carried several hundred eggs, from which tiny larvae hatched after 22 days, their size ranging from 1.8 to 1.9 millimetres. They were translucent and swam head-down in the water, moving backwards. Unfortunately they all died, probably not only due to the wrong kind of food, but apparently also because they were unable to moult without difficulty. It may be that these problems resulted from too much nitrate in the water, which should therefore be changed as

often as possible.

According to NG & CHIA (1994) the larvae develop in the estuaries of rivers and in the sea, but even under natural conditions only a few of the million of larvae hatched return to the rivers and highland brooks as fully developed shrimps. It must be emphasised that today's human pollution of the lower reaches of rivers represents an additional problem for the survival of these species.

Sometimes Atyopsis moluccensis *developes a very attractive red coloration.*

Shrimps
Palaemonids: Long-arm shrimps

Upper left: A pair of the longarm-shrimp from the Chocó in Western Colombia; the male is stopping a female.

Upper right: A young shrimp of the same species; you can see how these animals change when they get older.

Centre: Young Macrobrachium vollenhoveni from West-Africa (Lagos.

Below: This adult male of the Lagos Shrimp (Macrobrachium vollenhoveni) is lifting its claws in a threatening way.

Shrimps
Palaemonids: Long-arm shrimps

Palaemonids: Long-arm shrimps

The genus *Macrobrachium* (long-arm shrimps) belongs to a closely-related group of genera which also includes *Leander*, *Palaemonetes*, and *Palaemon*, which will be familiar, at least by name, to hobbyists specialising in marine aquaria. *Macrobrachium* live in rivers and are distributed all over the world, and there are so many species that it is almost impossible to identify them. More than 100 species have been described, and many more are as yet undescribed and perhaps still more not even discovered! Many look very similar, no matter whether they come from West Africa, Asia, Central or South America.

As well as the small species there are very large ones that attain a body length of 20 or even 30 centimetres. In their native countries they are prized as delicacies for the table and are hunted with spears, cast-nets, and even just bare hands. I must admit that I have caught and eaten several different species in Central America!

These long-arm shrimps are true freshwater animals which do not need to be kept in either brackish or hard water, and are sometimes found in habitats which are extremely poor in minerals, for example in regions where the delicate discus cichlid is also found. In Central America I have found these shrimps in water with a carbonate and general hardness of 6° to 18° dGH and KH. Temperatures vary, depending on geography and season, between 23 and 34°C, which means that these accommodating and hardy animals have no special requirements.

Nevertheless they will appreciate numerous hiding-places, e.g. among stones, plants and dead tree leaves used for decoration. In the wild, they utilise crannies between river boulders and are to be found among the thick layers of dead leaves that have fallen into the river, and are also fond of hiding in narrow cracks in the wood or beneath the bark of dead trees that have fallen into the water. There are, moreover, species which remain hidden for most of the day and come out only at feeding time or in the

Shrimps like to hide: This young Papaloapán-Shrimp has found shelter in a snail-shell.

Adult male of the Guinea Shrimp which is imported from West-Africa;

evening, and others which live on the bottom, but are quite active throughout the day, clambering all over the tank searching for anything edible. Yet others like to swim in the open water.

Most long-arm shrimps are not as colourful as the saltwater shrimps of the coral reefs, but more or less modestly coloured. They are nevertheless interesting by virtue of their bizarre faces with a long rostrum and greatly-projecting beady eyes positioned on so-called eye-stalks, and because of their long antennae and nimble, match-like, legs, the joints of which can be strikingly coloured - for example, red. It is really an amazing spectacle to watch these apparently motionless animals which in reality are almost constantly occupied cleaning themselves with their nearly invisible limbs. This "toilet" may produce an element of comedy: it is most amusing to see a short leg run across an eye like a hand, while at the same time the abdomen is bent forward and the animal starts scratching its posterior with another leg!

In the aquarium - a shallow tank with a volume of between 100 and 200 litres is quite adequate for keeping species which attain a body length of about 12 centimetres - these shrimps will have no problem finding individual "homes". Soon each will have selected its favourite place, which in most cases will be an elevated "perch" not far from shelter, from which it dexterously climbs down when you offer food!

As their natural food consists first and foremost of carrion, they above all like dead meaty material (frozen bloodworm and brine shrimp, chopped beef heart, fish, etc.). But they also readily eat manufactured food tablets, and should be given those that are vegetable-based, as in the wild these shrimps also eat decaying plant material, algae, and fresh young shoots. They skilfully seize these food tablets and turn them round in their short, brush-like hands, feeding on the tiny particles thus loosened. Some people keep these shrimps because they feed on algae, and are said to eat even the firmly-attached types, but at the same time do not harm higher plants. The amount of algae they eat depends, of course, on the species and number of shrimps – and it is foolish to expect miracles. In addition, most *Macrobrachium* will eat snails, and not only ramshorn snails, but also Malaysian live-bearing snails (*Melanoides*

tuberculata). It must also be borne in mind that some species pose a threat to small fishes, especially at night.

Like all other crustaceans they find their food by smell and approach it rapidly, excitedly feeling about with their antennae. Once they have taken their prey - which, if necessary, they vigorously defend against conspecifics or fishes - they carry it to a sheltered place. Not that they are at all timid - you will be able to observe them without difficulty most of the time. But they do fear competition from other occupants of the tank. These, by the way, shouldn't be too small. If you consider the size of your *Macrobrachium* and the fact that their generic name means "long-arm", not to mention the strong claws in which the arms terminate, then you can well imagine that they may take small fishes by surprise during the night although this is in fact rather rare - perhaps because it doesn't equate with their natural feeding behaviour. On the other hand they frequently fight with conspecifics and these quarrels often end in the loss of a leg or a claw, even though it is rare for one of the combatants to be killed. Plus, as already mentioned, lost limbs, will be replaced without problem at the next moult. A good supply of food and frequent water changes will encourage growth and the moulting this necessitates, and which they signal by stopping feeding and going into hiding. For this reason their tank should be provided with roots, stones, and plants, and not just for aesthetic reasons alone.

In addition these shrimps only seldom swim, and are thus hardly ever found in open water, instead leading a substrate-orientated life. They are skilful climbers, and where their legs cannot grip, they use their swimmerets for propulsion, gliding up the smooth vertical glass, so you should take care to cover their aquarium tightly. If danger threatens they stop for a moment, lifting their claws in a threatening manner. If they need to flee, they suddenly flick backwards, zigzagging away lightning-fast to safety.

The sexes of adult *Macrobrachium* are easily to determine, even at first glance, as the abdomen of the female is somewhat deeper: above the gizzard there is an egg chamber, in which – at least in transparent species - the eggs are clearly visible. In addition the sexes can also be distinguished by their claws: those of females are shorter and more slender, while those of the

Shrimps
Palaemonids: Long-arm shrimps

Upper left: Young Signal-stripe Shrimp are beautifully coloured.

Upper right: Adults get more or less brownish and lack the nice contrast of the strong yellow stripe on the black body.

Centre: This Macrobrachium-male was caught in the Papaloapán-drainage in Mexico.

Below: Macrobrachium rosenbergii from Malaysia is said to be the biggest long-arm shrimp in the world.
(Photo: E. Schraml)

Shrimps
Palaemonids: Long-arm shrimps

Beautifully yellow marked male of the Palenque Shrimp.

Females of the Palenque Shrimp get rather dark when they are carrying eggs.

(usually larger) males are variably elongated and thickened.

The function of these long arms in males, which are a secondary sexual characteristic, appears not to be connected – or only in part – with any need for enhanced weaponry in males. They may perhaps be used to demonstrate strength, but it is more likely that the long arms are used to manipulate females and thereby stimulate them to mate. Pairs of these shrimps can often be seen in a T-position, where the male approaches the female from the side and stops her, blocking her way forward with one claw, and retreat with the other.

Because *Macrobrachium* contains species in which males develop chelipeds of variable length and thickness, I have previously tried to categorise the species using this character. Unfortunately there are so many intermediate forms that the validity of this categorisation is questionable, and so I will here differentiate them only by the modes of reproduction already described on page 11, with the "swimming shrimps" (those that tend to swim in open water) as a third group.

The *Macrobrachium* of the primitive reproduc-

tive type can be bred only with difficulty in the aquarium, and then only in small numbers. You will be lucky to actually observe a mating. As a rule you will instead simply notice one day that the females are carrying numerous yellowish, orange, or greenish eggs around on the posterior abdomen, where they hang in close-packed masses between the swimmerets. The time taken for their development is 10 days to three weeks, depending on temperature and oxygen supply (water movement). The females then release innumerable tiny larvae, barely visible to the naked eye; in nature these would be carried by the current to brackish regions or the open sea, where they pass through numerous stages before returning to fresh water as fully-formed shrimps. They float head-down in the water and move with a hopping motion. Their eyes are large, but, unlike those of adults, immobile. Unfortunately it is rarely possible to provide them with suitable food, so that they usually survive only till about the fourth day and then die within a few eyes.

Preserved zoea larvae have been photographed with an electronic microscope by Dr. R. Riehl (University of Düsseldorf), whom I would like to thank for this favour. His pictures (see page 13) are very informative and show that the larvae lack pleopods at this stage and still use their forward-pointing walking legs (visible in the two upper photos), which are not yet completely developed, to move. They also already use their telson, whose broad "stem" is equipped with filigree "feathers", for jerky, hopping movement. The body is already armoured, and its posterior part segmented, as in adults, to facilitate movement. Their giant faceted eyes guarantee a wide field of vision. The larvae of *Macro-brachium* species are largely predatory, feeding on small planktonic organisms.

If the newly-released larvae are not too small, you can try to feed them with newly-hatched brine shrimp. In most cases this food will be too big, so that you will have to experiment with tinier items such as slipper animalcules, rotifers, micro-eels (*Panagrellus silusiae*), milk-powder (!), "Liquifry", or powdered flake food. With all of these you must be very careful that the water doesn't get cloudy and polluted, and it is best to install a small, air-powered sponge filter that will trap the finest particles without sucking in the tiny larvae.

Shrimps
Palaemonids: Long-arm shrimps

As has been already pointed out, the first moults can be a problem for Atyid larvae, and it seems that this is also the case for *Macrobrachium* larvae. Once released, they moult for the first time after 24 hours or so, and many of them die. Only those which survive for the first 14 days have a good chance of long-term survival: by this stage their initial whitish colour will be giving way to typical transparency, and by a size of about 12 millimetres the young will also have assumed the shape of their parents. At the same time they stop swimming around and start leading a substrate-orientated life, just as their parents do, i.e. they prefer to remain on the bottom or explore the decor.

The professional breeding of *Macrobrachium* species that produce tiny eggs, i.e. the primitive reproductive type, was first achieved a few years ago. Most experiments have involved *Macrobrachium rosenbergii*, said to be the largest freshwater shrimp in the world. Its size is the more remarkable in that it is an annual species in which males live for only a year (or a little more) and grow - if they are kept in large rearing ponds - to sizes of 200 to 220 mm, whereas females seldom live longer than a year and reach 180 to 200 mm. The growth rate slows down after five or six months and is better if the population density is lower and the temperature higher. In addition, the shrimps grow better if cultivated in fresh rather than brackish water. In the wild *M. rosenbergii* may attain up to 30 centimetres in males and 25.5 in females.

In experiments performed with other *Macrobrachium* species as well, it was subsequently ascertained that sexually mature males are always ready for copulation, whereas females have to moult before mating. It is believed that females also then secrete special scents that attract males.

Fresh eggs of *Macrobrachium rosenbergii* are mostly orange-coloured, but soon become darker, turning to a greyish-green and, just before hatching, nearly black. In 1961, in Malaysia, it was discovered that the larvae of *M. rosenbergii* survive only if they are kept in sufficiently saline water. If the larvae hatch in completely fresh water, they are doomed to die, even though the adult shrimps live in such water, more than 100 miles from the sea. In 1962 the first young shrimps were reared under laboratory conditions. Food size also seems to be significant: the particles must not be too small or the larvae will not accept them; on the other hand, they must not be too large either as the larvae will cling to them, sink to the bottom with them, and die there. For successfully raising larvae of *M. rosenbergii*, the food particles should be about one tenth of the body length of the larvae. They should be fed animal material, e.g. ground fish or egg yolk. At the same time, optimal water quality must be maintained and oxygen depletion avoided (Ling, 1977).

M. rosenbergii, which is native to Malaysia, seems to be the most suitable *Macrobrachium* species for commercial breeding, but a Tahitian species called *M. lar*, in which full- grown individuals can be found in brackish water, is also suitable for breeding, especially in places where fresh water is difficult to obtain or expensive. In America, *M. carcinus* and *M. ohione* are being bred successfully. Unfortunately, individuals of the first species are rather aggressive towards each other, so that they can't be kept in large numbers in small pools, but on the other hand they tolerate cooler water than *M. rosenbergii*. *M. ohione* is hardy, but grows slowly and is not large enough to eat, so that in Louisiana these shrimps are used for bait. *M. carcinus* and *M. acanthurus* are found in

Left: The Peacock Shrimp might be M. olfersi - here a male.

Right: Female of the Peacock Shrimp carrying eggs.

Shrimps
Palaemonids: Long-arm shrimps

Left: Males of the "Indian Shrimp I" develop extremely long arms.

Right: Femals carry small eggs. Their arms are considerably shorter and thinner.

Mexico, on the Atlantic slope in the Gulf of Mexico region, specifically in the federal states of Tamaulipas, Veracruz, Tabasco, and Campeche. On the Pacific slope there are two species, *M. americanum* and *M. tenellum*, which are distributed from Sinaloa in the north down to the frontier with Guatemala. The former species is more abundant in the north, the latter in the south. Other Mexican species, of little commercial interest, but which are nevertheless caught for food, are *M. olfersii*, *M. digueti*, *M. acanthochirus*, *M. michoacanus*, and *M. heterochirus* (see Hanson & Godwin, 1977).

Unlike the primitive species, all those that practice the specialised mode of reproduction are easy to breed in the aquarium. They produce large eggs, which may number up to a hundred and are light-coloured initially, subsequently becoming darker, almost black-brown. Depending on the species, water temperature, aeration, and water movement they develop over a period of three to six weeks during which the female – at least in some species – also becomes darker, so that it is not easy to detect that they are carrying eggs. It is advisable to isolate females carrying eggs after about two weeks.

Eventually they will release fully-formed young shrimps which can take *Artemia* nauplii and particles of flake or tablet food without difficulty, and grow on rapidly. During the first hours the mother remains with her young and guards them (?) – at any rate, cannibalism is non-existent or rare so that the brood can be reared without significant losses. They become sexually mature after only about three months.

The next few pages are devoted, by way of example, to some of the shrimps of the genus *Macrobrachium* that are imported for the aquarium hobby from Central and South America,

the Indian-Asian region, and Africa; in many cases the species names are unknown. The first of these is a so-called Guatemala Shrimp which I brought home from a Pacific-slope river in Central America, the Rio Maria Linda. Males grow to a total body length of nearly ten, females to about seven, centimetres. They are quite beautifully coloured: the amber body is ornamented with black-brown or reddish lines, sometimes bordered with yellow, and the joints of the legs and the brown arms and claws are red.

In the Rio Papaloapán basin on the Atlantic slope of southern Mexico lives a *Macrobrachium* species, the males of which can be a light blue, lighter on the belly and darker on the back. The tail fan is also dark. The undersides of the arms and legs are an intense blue, the claws brown. Young specimens are nearly colourless initially, later changing to a pale blue-grey, which is also the colour of adult females. This Papaloapán Shrimp lives a secretive life among the boulders of the river bottom. During the dry season the water is rather warm (27°C to 30°C), slightly alkaline (pH about 7.5) and medium hard (4 to 11°dGH; 4 to 13°KH). There is virtually no submerse vegetation.

In southern Mexico my friends and I found another, very attractively coloured shrimp in the rivers of the Atlantic slope from the Rio Papaloapán down to the Usumacinta. This species, the Signal-stripe Shrimp, has a short rostrum, with a broad, bright yellow longitudinal band running along the back and each side of the black body to the telson. The claws are also black, but at their base they have a prominent snow-white ring. We caught specimens of up to 17 cm body length. Unfortunately these large shrimps were not as intensely and contrastingly coloured as the young ones.

Shrimps
Palaemonids: Long-arm shrimps

Left: Male of the Papaloapán Shrimp

Left: This "Giant long-arm Shrimp" was caught among river boulders in Honduras. It might be identical with the "Signal-stripe Shrimp" (p. 27).

Right: This black Macrobrachium - the Cameroon Shrimp - has been imported from West-Africa.

Left: Male of the Jabuti Shrimp (Macrobrachium carcinus) from the Tapajós-drainage in Brazil.

Right: The Jabuti Shrimp develops long, but rather flat arms.

Right: Long-arm shrimps are considered very tasty in Central America. Even children try to catch them by any occasion.

Shrimps
Palaemonids: Long-arm shrimps

left: This shrimp of the specialized type of reproduction is imported from India. We call it the "Indian Shrimp II".

Right: The Ring-hand-Shrimp (Macrobrachium assamensis) has beautiful black and red ringed arms, which are a bit bigger in males.

Left: Females with eggs of this species get rather dark, so that you can't see the eggs well.

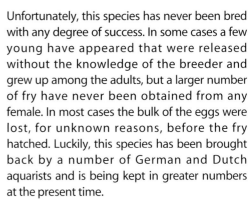

Right: The eggs of the Ring-hand-Shrimp are big; the young are completely developed when they hatch and can be raised easily.

In the Rio Otulum (in the Grijalva drainage), near the world-famous ruins of Palenque in southern Mexico, I found another *Macrobrachium* which is probably as yet undescribed. The males of this Palenque Shrimp develop stronger and longer chelipeds than the females, but both sexes have an attractive black and yellow colour pattern. Males grow a little larger than females and attain a body length of about four centimetres. The deeper-bodied females grow to only about 3.5 centimetres.

The water in the natural habitat is hard with a pH of about 7.5, and the temperature varies seasonally from slightly above to a little below 25°C. These shrimps can be kept in an aquarium of about 30 litres. When they are fully grown they look as if they are covered with brown powder, with the fine spots on the carapace creating a dark marbled pattern. The colour pattern also includes black lines and a light longitudinal band on the back. Depending on age and condition, females of this species lay between 20 and 60 rather large eggs, from which hatch larvae that continue to feed on the remains of their yolk sac for a few days. After about three weeks they measure about four millimetres, by which time they are fully-formed, resembling their parents, and begin independent life.

Unfortunately, this species has never been bred with any degree of success. In some cases a few young have appeared that were released without the knowledge of the breeder and grew up among the adults, but a larger number of fry have never been obtained from any female. In most cases the bulk of the eggs were lost, for unknown reasons, before the fry hatched. Luckily, this species has been brought back by a number of German and Dutch aquarists and is being kept in greater numbers at the present time.

In northern South America, in western Colombia – the so-called Chocó - I found another species in totally fresh water that was clear, mineral-depleted (0°dGH, 3-3.5°KH), with a pH of 5.5 to 6 and a temperature of about 27°C. I brought back some young of this Chocó Shrimp from another brook in the Baudo drainage, near Pie de Pepé. At a size of some three centimetres they are more or less amber-coloured and translucent, but strikingly decorated with brown

Shrimps
Palaemonids: Long-arm shrimps

Left: Male of the Volta Shrimp that has been imported from Ghana.

Right: female of the Volta Shrimp.

Left: Males of the Zaire Shrimp develop extremely loing arms.

Right: The Zaire Shrimp - here a female - can be beautifully marbled.

lines. Their arms are slender at this time, seeming rather fragile, but the appearance of these shrimps changes noticeable over time and from moult to moult.

Males grow more quickly and develop long, strong, arms and claws, while both sexes become increasingly darker until they are almost completely brownish-red. The rostrum is darker than the rest, the cephalothorax a little lighter, the abdomen nearly black. An irregularly-edged light band extends along the posterior part of the body. The central part of the tail fan is again dark, while the uropods are reddish-brown. The arms are dark on the underside, lighter above. The claws themselves are dark brown.

Males appear to be fully grown at about 12 centimetres, and the length of their arms may exceed the length of the body. Females attain a size of about seven centimetres. Their arms are thinner and noticeably shorter. It is difficult to say whether they are also less effective as offensive weapons. It may be that the long chelipeds of the males are something of a hindrance in fights and to mobility in general,

and, of course, they break off easily. At any rate females seem to be more agile. And even in the confines of the aquarium - I kept my shrimps in pairs in tanks with a capacity of 120 litres (75 x 40 x 40 cm) - the males never harmed the females.

The rather glassy Peacock Shrimp, which has a shiny yellow back, may be *Macrobrachium olfersii*. The natural distribution of this species comprises large areas of Central and South America, but since 1933 it has also been found in Florida, where it was - perhaps not deliberately - introduced by man. It attains a body length of 7 to 9 centimetres - males being invariably larger than females of the same age. Adult specimens are recognisable by a narrow, dark-brown band and a dark blotch on both of the outer wings of the tail fan. These blotches are not present: in young specimens, or only faintly to be seen, and they may fade in adults if these are in poor health. Only adult females have attractive black and white markings along the angled rims of the lower abdomen. The eggs of this species are light green initially and change colour to grey as they develop. The larvae can supposedly be raised in fresh water.

Left: The Cuban-Shrimp develops one oversized arm.
(Photo: M. Keijman)

Right: Young Chamaeleon-Shrimps (Macrobrachium scabriculum) are most often bluish.

Left: Adult males of the Chamaeleon-Shrimp develop a cushion of bristles around the oversized arm.

Right: Male of a long-arm shrimp from Panama, the males of which develop one very strong arm; the species spawns tiny eggs.

Left: M. lanchesteri has two rather small arms.
(Photo: W. A. Tomey)

Right: This shrimp with one strongly developed arm was erroneously sold under the name of M. lanchesteri. (Photo: J. Pinhard / Archiv A.C.S.)

Left: Shrimp with a giant left arm from western Ecuador.

Right: This female carries tiny eggs. It was found at the same place, but it is not sure that it belongs to the same species.

Shrimps
Palaemonids: Long-arm shrimps

During an expedition to Brazil I found other long-arm shrimps in the lower basin of the Tapajós and in the Amazon south of Santarém. The small rivers or brooks that cross the road to Colonia Jabuti were teeming with waterlilies and other, submerse, plants. In places the banks were densely bordered with reeds and other marsh plants. The river bottom was soft, consisting of sand or a thick layer of rotten leaves and wood. The biotope conditions were thus quite different from the stony rivers of Central America, and, of course, the water chemistry was different too. The water was tea-coloured and clear, with a pH of about 5.5 and no measurable general or carbonate hardness. And yet we found an amazing abundance of freshwater crustaceans in these waters.

This brownish or brown-red shrimps, which I called Jabuti Shrimps in the first edition of this book, have been identified by S. De Grave as *Macrobrachium carcinus*. This species is distributed over large parts of eastern America, from Florida down to southern Brazil, and lives in both fresh and brackish water. Males grow to about 23, females to sizes between 13 and 17 centimetres. The body is rather stout, both chelipeds being extremely long in males, with especially broad, strong forearms. Both sexes develop a rather beautiful reddish colour over time, and a light stripe appears on the outer sides of the chelipeds. In addition, there is a lighter spot on the head and a whitish or yellowish ring round the base of the tail fan. Unfortunately these shrimps did not breed in my tanks, so I have no knowledge of their reproductive behaviour.

The ring-hand shrimp most commonly kept in the aquarium, which is one of the specialised breeders, has now been identified by S. DE GRAVE as *Macrobrachium assamensis*. The species was described from the Someswari River in the Garo Hills and is said to occur in the eastern Himalaya region, in the Chota Nagpur tract, and the Satpuras in India, and also in hilly regions of Burma (now Myanmar), but not the lowland plains. There are two subspecies, *M. assamensis assamensis* and *M. assamensis peninsularis*. The popular name refers to the arms in juveniles, which are red with black spots so that they look as if they are wearing striped socks. This is not, however, a reliable character, and, of course, these shrimps too change in the course of their lives: youngsters are initially glassy transparent, with lines visible on the body; later a brown marbling develops. In adults the large spots may be surrounded by light dots, while the armour is brownish. Individual specimens are sometimes bright red in colour. The clawed arms of males are not particularly long, but thickened. The species attains a body length of some 5 (females) to 7 (males) centimetres, is exceptionally adaptable, and can be bred without problems.

Another shrimp of the specialised reproductive type, which grows a little larger than the Ring-hand Shrimp has been imported from India and has already been bred under aquarium conditions. Females of this "Indian Shrimp" are light-coloured, with a number of bluish-grey or dark olive stripes and blotches. Innumerable tiny silvery dots are to be found all over the body. Males grow to a larger size, have longer and slightly thicker arms, and adopt a dark coloration consisting of black-olive elements as soon as they become dominant. The arms and claws are almost completely black, and the posterior part of the body is dark marbled. Breeding poses no difficulties, but note that the species seems to be rather aggressive towards conspecifics.

Besides this species there is a second Indian Shrimp which practices the primitive mode of reproduction and which also grows - depending on sex - to about 5 or 7 centimetres body length. The chelipeds of the females are short and thin, those of the males extremely long. In addition, adult females have attractive alternating black and white markings along the angled rims of the lower abdomen - a colour pattern that is also found in females of other *Macrobrachium* species.

Another small *Macrobrachium* species, probably adapted to a life on sandy bottoms, is sold as *Macrobrachium* "luzifugem". It originates from India and has a greenish to brownish body with irregular fine white marbling - and hence is perfectly camouflaged over a sandy bottom. Its claws are small and measure no more than a third of the length of the carapace. Females are smaller and attain about 35 mm body length. They are more sturdily built than males, which grow up to 45 mm. This species can be kept at temperatures around 25°C and a pH value of about 7. It doesn't matter if the water is hard, but these shrimps do react badly to sudden changes in water parameters. They are also said to be rather shy and timid, so plenty of hiding-places are desirable. The females produce a small number (15-20) of large eggs, and the young are said to be relatively easy to rear.

Young *Macrobrachium* are also found from time to time among ornamental fish imports from western Africa. The arms and legs of the species known as the Guinea Shrimp are brownish (or brownish-marbled) like the body, and its claws are comparatively broad. This species grows to a body length of about 13 centimetres. Unfortunately nothing is known about its true identity.

The *Macrobrachium* species from India known as the Red-spotted Shrimp grows rather large - the specimen illustrated grew from about 5 to 15 cm long in the course of a year. It is found in the Ichamati river in Bengal, about 40 km from Calcutta.

From Ghana I brought home another *Macrobrachium*, here called the Volta Shrimp, after its river of origin. It is more or less transparent, even though its body is covered in tiny dark dots, producing an overall dusky appearance. However, most of the time these shrimps appear translucent-brown or reddish-brown , with a dark back and brown chelipeds, along whose outer edge runs a light stripe which continues on the lower finger of the claw. The chelipeds are long, but little thickened, so that the species looks rather delicate. In males the arms are about a third longer than in females, which makes it easy to determine the sexes. This

shrimp produces small eggs.

By contrast, large eggs are laid by a *Macrobrachium* shrimp from Zaire, here simply called the Zaire Shrimp. These animals are glassy-yellow when young, but soon a fine dark speckling appears, alternating with brown blotches and creating an attractive marbled pattern. Breeding females in particular are dark, and their chelipeds almost black. The latter are short and thin, whereas those of the males are extremely long. Unfortunately, I haven't been able managed to breed this species successfully so far. I had two females which both carried eggs for some time, but one lost her eggs and the other died for unknown reasons before releasing her fry.

In specialist pet-shops you will quite often find the so-called Lagos Shrimp. It is imported from Nigeria (Lagos) and can be found in Ghana as well, maybe elsewhere. In the past, it was wrongly referred to as the Laos Shrimp and taken for an Asian species! D. Brandis has identified this species as *Macrobrachium vollenhoveni* (pers. comm.).

It grows to about 20 centimetres body length and develops especially long arms which are thicker in males than in females, but nevertheless slender and covered with small warty growths and somewhat larger spines. Along the upper edge of the arms there is a regular row of such spines. On top of the rostrum there are about a dozen very pointed serrae (saw-teeth), and five on the underside. The claws are brilliant blue, while their bases and the ends of the forearms are yellow in young individuals. The

The Red-spotted Shrimp is a large species from fresh water in Bengal, and is imported for the aquarium hobby. (Photo: F. Schäfer)

Shrimps
Palaemonids: Long-arm shrimps

rest of the arms is bluish in older specimens, and the upper edge of the otherwise grey forearm is yellow.

Females of this species grow to at least 15 centimetres. Their chelipeds are narrower and smaller in cross-section, but almost as long as those of the males. The numerous eggs are orange-coloured initially and so small that there seems little hope of breeding these shrimps successfully under aquarium conditions. Their size alone dictates an aquarium of about 200 litres with a bottom area of about 100 x 60 or 120 x 50 centimetres for a group of three or four of these giant shrimps. In contrast to smaller species there is also a greater risk that they will prey on fishes, seizing them with their claws. Of course they will find it easier to catch fishes that are ill or cultivated forms with long tails that are not able to flee fast enough, and during the night they may take sleeping fishes by surprise. In addition they eat a considerable amount of food: within a few minutes an adult specimen can shovel down three smelt (slender food fish, about 5 centimetres long, available frozen – but defrost before use).

There are also long-arm shrimps of a quite different type in which males develop only one oversized arm. I have found such shrimps in different parts of South America, for example in western Ecuador, but I must admit that I am not quite sure if the males and females I caught at the same place represent the same species. The females were carrying numerous very small eggs, so it doesn't seem likely that they can be bred under aquarium conditions.

This is also true of a species I have provisionally called the Chamaeleon Shrimp, which was previously believed to be *Macrobrachium pilimanus*. According to De Grave (pers. comm.), it is not in fact that species but *M. scabriculum*, a shrimp which is distributed in Sri Lanka, southern India, Singapore, and the Malaysian peninsula (including Tioman). There are other, older, suspect reports that the species also occurs in East Africa and Madagascar. The species is purportedly similar to *M. dolichodactylus*, a species which can be found in the same areas – and in East Africa!

In addition, *M. scabriculum* bears an unmistakeable resemblance, both morphologically and in its coloration, to the so-called Cuban Shrimp

that M. Keijman brought to Europe from the northeast part of that Caribbean island.

In juvenile shrimps of this type the chelipeds are slender and both the same length. In the course of time, one of the arms becomes longer and thicker - this is also true of females, even though their enlarged arm always remains significantly smaller than that of the male. Fine bristles then gradually develop around the forearm of the latter, forming a kind of cuff-like cushion, from which the claws emerge. Unfortunately nothing is known about the function of this cushion.

It should be added that the upper parts of the arms of adult specimens, the entire smaller arm, and all the anterior limbs (except the antennae and the walking legs) are covered with conspicuous long bristles, resembling spines.

It seems appropriate to call this species the Chamaeleon Shrimp, because it too can vary its colours considerably. In juvenile specimens both the body and the legs are sometimes marbled light brown , but more often greyish-blue to sky blue, the darker spots on the body intensifying with age, forming discrete, increasingly darker blotches which are black-brown in adult specimens. Full-grown shrimps also exhibit a yellow-brown stripe which runs from the rostrum along the carapace to the telson and which broadens from head to tail. On the upper side of the tail this stripe may be divided into two parallel parts. The edges of the tail fan and the upper carapace may also be adorned with lighter streaks.

These shrimps lead a very secretive "subterranean" life, i.e. they normally choose a narrow retreat near the bottom, for example under a stone or a root, which they then excavate, carrying and pushing sand and fine gravel to the exit. This may explain the cushion of bristles around the thickened arm - protection when the latter is used for shifting sand. When the work is done, they spend most of their time peering from these dugouts, waiting for food, which they seize in a quick dart, hurrying back to their caves immediately afterwards.

Their method of reproduction is that of the less specialised species, producing very small eggs from which, after eight to ten days, hatch tiny larvae which are virtually impossible to raise under aquarium conditions.

Palaemonids: Long-arm shrimps

There are other shrimps (with rather short arms) which are here termed "swimming shrimps", rather than "floating shrimps" as previously, because that name is used for the species of the family Mysidaceae. Some of these may also have been imported, but that is not definite. The swimming shrimp have in fact been imported as Ghost Shrimps from South and Central America, India, and Africa (Guinea, Zaire) and practice - as far as we know to date - the primitive mode of reproduction. Most of them are small, always transparent, almost invisible shrimps lacking any markings. Even in a well-decorated aquarium they prefer to remain in the darkest corners - it is obvious that they avoid the light.

During the night their behaviour changes: they come out of hiding, paddle about in the open water using their comparatively long swimmerets, and search for food, which in nature supposedly consists of tiny plankton. For this reason you can feed them on brine shrimp nauplii, powdered flake food, or fine frozen food (for example *Cyclops*). Naturally you must put the food into the tank a while after switching off the light. You should also take care that the food is distributed and circulated by the aeration, because these crustaceans catch their food in the open water. This also means that they lead a less substrate-oriented life than many of their relatives.

These "swimming shrimps" are highly specialised in various ways: firstly, their eyes are extraordinarily large, which undoubtedly enables them to orientate effectively, even in the dark. Secondly, their swimmerets are extremely long. They paddle forward with almost imperceptible movements, such that they seem to float. In fact, in West Africa there are swimming shrimps that can even swim on the spot, with their swimmerets bent at 90° to their sides! If they swim fast, their movements sometimes seem rather clumsy. But in the event of danger they flee as fast as lightning, shooting away backwards with their tail fans spread wide and jerky contractions of their abdomens.

Their transparency must also be regarded as a protective specialisation. And finally, all these species have fine, iridescent lines on the antennae and on the back. These are produced by chromatophores and enable the shrimps to recognise each other and to keep close together, as they apparently live in large shoals in nature. This is, at least, what hobbyists have observed in Central America: Garbe (pers. comm.) was unable to take photos of fishes while diving in Cuban mountain rivers during the night because there were too many swimming shrimps, which had not been visible during the daytime. Schaller (pers. comm.) reports similar experiences in Madagascar.

These shrimps react with panic when the light is switched on suddenly, and this means that they may jump through the smallest gaps in aquarium cover glasses. It is therefore strongly recommended hat all openings, e.g. for the air supply, filter pipework, and/or electricity cables, should be blocked with filter floss/foam or similar.

One of these swimming shrimps is imported from India. It grows to a little more than four centimetres and, as its transparent carapace exhibits a bluish shimmer, it is here called the Blue Indian Shrimp. Sometimes a yellowish blotch is visible inside the body behind the neck, but this can disappear completely. The edges of the segments of the abdominal armour are dark, creating a pattern of vertical bands..

The sexes are easy to distinguish in that the angled edges of the caudal segments are darker in the deeper-bodied females than in males. The pleopods are long, especially in males, and angled forwards, so that when the shrimp swims forward, their tips are often curved backwards. And these shrimps not only like to swim a lot, but do so forwards as often as backwards. The females lay small, bright yellow eggs from which hatch tiny larvae.

The swimming shrimps also include a small species, originating from Paraguay, which is the first freshwater shrimp to be seen performing cleaner behaviour, previously known only from marine species. Further study of this phenomenon is required, but an armoured catfish seemed very happy to be tended by the barely 3 cm long shrimp.

Shrimps
Palaemonids: Long-arm shrimps

Left: This "swimming-shrimp" from Guinea can be found in the open water, especially during the night.

Right: The same species keeps hidden among the plants during the daytime.

*Left: Clear for all to see: a small swimming shrimp from Paraguay cleaning an armoured catfish.
(Photo: F. Schäfer).*

Right: Macrobrachium sp. "luzifugem" - its identity is still unclear - is merely to be seen on a sandy bottom.

The Blue Indian Shrimp seems to be a swimming-shrimp, too.

Tropical crayfish species are the most suitable for aquarium maintenance, and European species are only very rarely maintained. In the first instance this is because all our native crays are strictly protected, so that only species bred for the table or imported are available. Secondly, it must be borne in mind that coldwater species cannot kept in warm water all the time. They need a winter rest period, during which the water temperature should drop to - depending on the species in question - well below 10°C and must be at this low level for several weeks at least. Unfor-

tunately, there are no low-priced cooling units available for this purpose, whereas it is, on the other hand, quite inexpensive and easy to heat an aquarium. A third reason is that our native crays do not exhibit much activity during the winter time, retiring to their hiding-places and rendering the aquarium devoid of living interest.

Nevertheless it is important to be aware that three native European species do exist: *Astacus astacus*, *Austropotamobius torrentium*, and *A. pallipes*, the last of which is the only species found in Great Britain. The first of these is reputedly very tasty and was distributed all over central Europe, with exception of the mountainous regions, during the 18th century. Unfortunately its numbers were much reduced by the crayfish pestilence, and today it is considered an endangered species. *Austropotamobius torrentium* lives in mountainous areas, but is of no commercial importance. This is also true of *A. pallipes*.

Astacus leptodactylus, the Galician Swamp Cray, is occasionally imported from eastern Europe. It can be blue or brownish-olive in colour, with the underside the same colour as the rest of the body. Its claws are long and slender, and its body covered in spines, and it has post-orbital processes on the upper side of the carapace, behind the eyes. *A. leptodactylus* has two of these humps, just like *Astacus astacus*. Males are easily recognisable by their gonopods, and females by the genital openings at the base of the second pair of walking legs. Females remain considerably smaller, are more sturdily built, and have a broader tail and smaller claws than males. The latter may grow to 18 centimetres body length and can weigh more than 200 grams.

This species owes its popular name to its natural range, namely Galicia, the northern slope and foothills of the Carpathians, a region that today belongs mainly to Poland. But this cray is also found in other eastern European countries and in Turkey. It is unclear whether its natural range also includes eastern Austria or if it was introduced there by Man. Its presence in Germany is also attributable to Man.

There are four subspecies, which sometimes also live in brackish water! The species

One cannot discuss imported American crayfishes without warning that they represent a danger to our European crayfishes (*Astacus astacus*, *Potamobius torencium*, *Austropotamobius pallipes*) because they can infect them with the so-called "crayfish pestilence", a mycosis which was unknown in Europe until about 100 years ago when the "Camber crayfish" (*Orconectes limosus*) was released in our waters. As our native crayfishes had no means of coping with the alien virus or fungus spores, large numbers of them died. Indeed, they even died out completely in many areas - only isolated populations survived. And this happened not only in Germany, but also in France, Spain, Sweden, Finland and - during the eighties - apparently also in Turkey. At the same time, American crayfishes conquered the natural habitats of the native species, and since then have made it impossible to re-establish the original species again. As the American crayfishes are constantly infested with mycosis spores, all such experiments are doomed to failure. That is why we have to be extremely careful that no American crayfish escapes and gets into our home waters, so that you must abandon any idea of keeping American crays in your garden pond or releasing them in lakes, brooks, or rivers. Even the water from tanks occupied by American crayfishes for some time should not be disposed of with other waste water - you need to boil it first.

Left: Two Galician Swamp Crays threatening each other.

Right: Male of the Galician Swamp Cray; the picture shows the gonopods.

Center: Our River Cray (Astacus astacus) has been nearly eradicated by the cray-pestilence that has been introduced by American crayfishes.

Below: The Galician Swamp Cray develops mighthy claws.

tolerates temperatures between 7 and 22°C (up to 30°C for short periods) and can be kept and bred only in spacious aquaria. These crays feed on any edible material, including autumn leaves, thread algae, aquatic plants, snails, and aquatic insects. These mainly crepuscular – or completely nocturnal – crays are only slightly aggressive among themselves. Mating occurs in autumn at water temperatures of about 10 to 12°C. The up to 400 eggs are laid some hours, or sometimes, up to 14 days, after copulation. Their development rate is largely dependent on the prevailing temperature.

Large American species

A small number of North American crayfishes belong to the subfamily Astacinae and the genus *Pacifastacus*. Only one of these, *Pacifastacus leniusculus*, has reached Europe, where it is known as the Signal Cray. It owes its popular name to the white joints of its claws, but the red underside of the claws is very conspicuous too. The species grows to about 15 centimetres and is sometimes also called the Californian River Cray. In the 1960s this cray was introduced into waters in Sweden, Great Britain, France, Spain, Finland, Poland, and Russia and has spread further within in those countries.

Adult specimens feed almost exclusively on vegetable material. They are long-lived crays, the males of which do not reach maturity until they are a year and a half old. In females, maturity is said to be attained even later, at the age of about two and a half years, and the incubation of their eggs is cited as up to 6 months or more. In Germany the species mates at the end of October, and the young hatch in May. It is not really suitable for aquarium maintenance, as it needs to be kept at low temperatures (not exceeding 15°C), which can cause problems, at least in the summer time.

The other Central and North American crays belong to the subfamily Cambarinae which comprises about 300 different species! These are assigned to the genera *Cambarus*, *Fallicambarus*, *Faxonella*, *Hobbseus*, *Orconectes*, *Procambarus*, and *Troglocambarus*. They include large and small, aggressive and peaceful species, and both extreme plant-eaters and others that do not harm higher plants at all. They also come from different climatic zones, which means that their temperature requirements vary considerably. There is thus little point in generalising too much. Even so, general statements can be made regarding the nutritional requirements of these crays (and all the other crayfishes discussed later). As they feed on carrion in the wild, their food needn't be "fresh". They voraciously devour the flesh of fish or mussels, as well as food tablets. They also readily accept any kind of frozen or commercially produced fish food (fish eggs, *Mysis*, bloodworm, sticks, pellets) and greedily feed on vegetable matter (frozen lettuce, spinach, Brussels sprouts). They also like to nibble on some types of twigs or branches (willow, alder, oak, beech) and leaves (those of beeches and oaks are said to prevent mycosis). They should also be given material they can use for shell-building, for example in-shell shrimps or coarse-cut fish complete with scales and bones.

At present probably only one *Orconectes* species is available for aquarium purposes, namely the Camber Cray, *Orconectes limosus*, originally described as *Cambarus affinis*, which grows to about 11 centimetres. The genus name is derived from the Greek and means "barrel-shaped swimmer", while the specific name is Latin, meaning "of mud", alluding to the natural habitat (swampy areas). Like other *Orconectes* it has a "warty" dorsal carapace, spines on the sides of the head, and a postorbital ridge behind the eye. The striking brownish-red, vertically-elongate, blotches on the individual segments of the abdomen are a further diagnostic character. The tips of the claws may be studded with orange-red spines. The species inhabits Atlantic slope drainages of North America from Maine south to the lower James River in Virginia. The Camber Cray was introduced into German rivers in 1890, and has subsequently conquered large parts of the drainages of the Rhine and Main, as well as rivers in Lower Saxony, and is now found in rivers, canals, lakes, and reservoirs. These crayfishes survive our winters and can thus be kept in a garden pond - but only if there is absolutely no way they can escape. In any case, it is better to keep them in a cool tank. The water temperature can be allowed to rise to about 25°C or more for short periods in summer. That apart, these crayfishes appreciate hard water with an alkaline pH (above 7.2), and prefer a coarse gravel or pebble bottom rather than sand, with numerous caves and clean, well-filtered water.

North world crayfishes
Large American species

Adult male of the Camber-Cray Orconectes limosus.

Beautifully red specimen of the Louisiana Swamp-Cray Procambarus clarkii.

There are also more or less blue specimens of this species.

Upper left: Male of the Cuban cray, Procambarus cubensis.

Upper right: Mating of the Cuban cray - a young one watching the scene.

Center: A look below the abdomen of a female Cuban cray that is carrying larvae.

Below: Young Cuban crays are often quite bluish.

North world crayfishes
Large American species

Orconectes limosus is also constantly active during the daytime. By dint of moulting, males alternate between two forms, a sexually active and a sexually inactive one. The former can most readily be recognised by its enlarged claws. In addition, such males have so-called ischium-hooks on the third element of the middle pair of walking legs which they use to anchor themselves to females. There are as yet no reports of successful reproduction under aquarium conditions, though breeding should be possible. In the wild, mating occurs in late autumn, but the females do not lay their 100 to 300, perhaps even 600, eggs until spring. The larvae hatch after four to six weeks and are carried about by their mother, metamorphosing through two different stages (which shouldn't be fed) into fully-formed crays, which then finally start to live independently.

A. Nolte brought back a crayfish from the Mississippi south of Jackson which may be an *Orconectes* species, too. Its body is unspotted, but its carapace is marked with two broad, curved, bluish-grey bands. The first marks the posterior edge of the head, the second runs along the entire posterior edge of the cephalothorax. The face, too, is bluish-grey, and the segments of the abdomen and the tail fan are delineated with brown. The most conspicuous characters are, however, the bright red spots behind the eyes, sometimes also on the back, the red tips of the claws, and red markings on the middle joints of the walking legs.

Most of the American crayfish sold in pet shops are members of the genus *Procambarus*. A species worth recommending is the Cuban Cray, *Procambarus cubensis*. It grows to about 8 or 10 centimetres and can be quite variably coloured, and its colour also changes as it grows. Most young ones are an attractive sky blue, medium-sized specimens are greyish-blue to greyish-brown, and older individuals are usually a uniform pale reddish brown. The form shown here is the subspecies *P. cubensis cubensis* which is found in the Cuban lowlands. Its carapace is smooth and without spines, with two longitudinal postorbital ridges behind the eye grooves, a short rostrum with a single point, and slender claws.

The Cuban Cray is not very aggressive. When first introduced into an aquarium, these crays will, of course, fight for their caves, but the quarrelling is soon over. Within their caves, they are find shelter in a strategically favourable spot which they create, at least in part, themselves, using sand, gravel and even pieces of wood to erect a wall, over which they are just able to see what is going on outside. If two crays meet in the aquarium, they may raise their claws in threat, but in most cases the weaker individual retreats from the field of battle without any conflict taking place. In a real fight the weaker crayfish may be thrown onto its back. If it is expedient to flee, it jerks backwards, whipping its tail forward, zigzagging lightning-fast to safety. But if the crayfishes know each other well, this happens only rarely. It should be added that the females are by no means afraid of the males, perhaps because they are bigger and quite capable of repulsing attacks and unwanted advances on the part of males.

The Cuban Crayfish can be used as an example of how to distinguish the sexes in crayfishes of the genus *Procambarus*. There are at least some species – including the Cuban Cray, - in which the claws are so similar in all individuals that they do not indicate the sex reliably. Nevertheless the entire body of the male, and above all the abdomen, is more slender, and the claws seem to be longer - this can be seen more easily from above. Secondly, the males have so-called "ischium-hooks", about one millimetre long, on the fourth element of the third pair of walking legs (counting from the front) (males of *P. clarkii* have these hooks on the second and third pairs of walking legs). The third distinguishing feature is the gonopods, which are to be found behind the last pair of legs. The first and second pleopods in males form a kind of "stirrup (petasma), consisting of a right and a left "arm", both of which are directed forward and are used to transfer the sperm. Females lack these, but between the last and the second-last pair of their walking legs there is a whitish, oval plate with a diameter of 2-3 millimetres, termed the annulus ventralis, and which is a characteristic of all the Cambaridae. In males it is so small as to be virtually invisible.

The breeding behaviour of the American crayfishes can also be exemplified by the Cuban Crayfish. Mating often takes place following a water change. The male grasps the female and turns her onto her back, with the female indicating her readiness to mate by becoming rigid. During the act of copulation, which takes about

North world crayfishes
Large American species

Procambarus geodytes *is always at work, digging in the sand.*

Pacifastacus leniusculus, *the Signal Cray originates in North America. It can be identified by it´s white markings at the claws.(Photo: Sch. Nakano/Archiv A.C.S.)*

ten minutes, both partners remain completely motionless and then separate without showing any further interest in each other.

Females with eggs can be transferred to another aquarium without hesitation. The eggs are round, with a diameter of about 1.5 to 2.0 millimetres, and hang like "bunches of grapes" of varying sizes beneath the abdomen, to which they are firmly attached. Their number ranges from 100 to 150, maybe even 300, but often not all of them develop for some reason, and are lost. They are greyish-green initially, but by the second or third day their colour will already have changed to a dark brown with a lighter "tip". Breeding females wave their pleopods to and fro, the more frequently the less the aquarium water is aerated. Well-oxygenated water seems important for the optimal development of the eggs. The future mother also keeps hidden most of the time, eating nothing. After 14 days the first newly-hatched young can be seen, still attached to the abdomen of their mother, leaving her by and by. The incubation time of the eggs depends largely on the prevailing conditions –

17 days at 26°C , and 25 at 20 to 22°C. It takes another three or four other days for all the young crayfishes to leave their mother. The female does not hunt them for food, nor does she start feeding again until she has been put back with her adult conspecifics.

The size of the young is about three millimetres initially, and they can easily be raised. As they don't show much interest in vegetarian food during the first weeks, it is best to offer them live brine shrimp nauplii, which they catch dexterously. After feeding, the orange-coloured shrimps can be seen inside their translucent bodies. They will also eat microworm, *Cyclops*, and Grindal worm. They must have food constantly available as otherwise they will try to eat each other. As they grow quickly, there are always some that have just moulted, and it is difficult to provide enough hiding-places to prevent cannibalism completely. At the age of about four weeks the young will already have attained a length of over two centimetres and exhibit a beautiful blue coloration.

The American crayfish that is seen and offered most frequently in pet shops is undoubtedly *Procambarus clarkii*. Its popular name is the Louisiana Swamp Crayfish, reflecting its provenance and its natural habitat. But the species is also distributed in many other southern states of the USA and some of the northern states of Mexico. There are bright red, reddish-brown, and bluish forms of this species, which - in spite of its beautiful colours - cannot be recommended without a warning: these crayfish not only grow to about 20 centimetres, but they will also destroy and eat any plants and defend a large territory vigorously, so that young specimens are best reared in separate tanks. If you put a number of them into the same aquarium, the strongest individual will grow faster than the rest and kill the others one by one, ending up as the sole survivor. On the other hand, in suitably spacious tanks you can keep adult specimens in the company of large fishes (e.g. cichlids) if you provide enough hiding-places. This species is undemanding and adaptable and will tolerate cold (down to15°C) and rather warm (up to 28°C) water for short periods. In summer they should be kept at about 23° - 24°C, and at a lower temperature during the winter time. The water should not be too mineral-poor, and a little salt should be added. The reproductive behaviour of this species is similar to that of *P. cubensis*.

North world crayfishes
Large American species

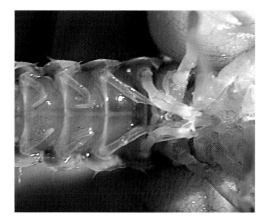

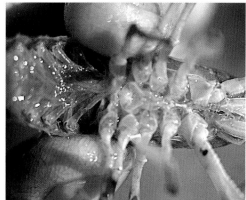

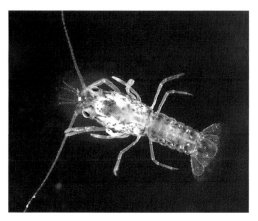

From C. Lukhaup I obtained some *Procambarus geodytes*, a species in which the males have hooks on the third and fourth pairs of legs, and which is distributed along the St. John's River from Putnam County to Orange County in Florida, preferring - like *P. alleni* - marshy or swampy areas that dry up periodically. If the water level drops, they stay more or less where they are and dig deep burrows. These are easy to find because the crays throw up chimney-like funnel-shaped entrances. They then remain at the bottom of their burrows where it is cool and sufficiently moist that they do not dry out or suffocate. They also mate and lay their eggs underground, and do not emerge until it starts to rain again. They then migrate overland, searching for water in which to release their young before going their separate ways.

Procambarus leonensis is also native to Florida, where it inhabits slow-flowing or stagnant waters in the drainages of the rivers Apalachicola and Suwannee. Its habitus is similar to that of *P. clarkii*, as is its attractive coloration. Where aquarium maintenance is concerned, it seems that this *Procambarus* species at least will not tolerate long-term high temperatures (about 30°C).

Procambarus alleni, the Blue Florida Cray, can be recognised by its spotted, "warty" shell. It grows to at least 12 centimetres body length and can be extremely variable in coloration: it is mostly vivid blue or bluish-violet specimens that are imported, but there are also inconspicuous bluish and brown individuals. The species is distributed east of the St. John's River and throughout the Florida peninsula south of Levy and Marion counties, and inhabits slow-flowing brooks, quiet shallow waters, and swampy regions, which means that, just like *P. geodytes*, it lives a semi-terrestrial life, i.e. sometimes out of water. In the aquarium these crays tolerate temperatures between 15 and 28°C, but the optimal temperature range is supposedly 20 - 27°C. The pH of the water should be alkaline and lie between 7.5 and 8. On the other hand the hardness of the water plays only an insignificant role. It is, nevertheless, important that the water is free of copper, nitrates, and other organic toxins, adequately circulated or aerated, and subject to regular partial changes.

Procambarus milleri, the Tangerine Cray, is also native to Florida, but is troglodytic, that is to say it lives in subterranean watercourses in lime-

North world crayfishes
Large American species

und 30°C (but don't keep it too warm in the long term!) and grows to about 8 centimetres; both sexes develop claws of a similar size. It has already been bred, and a single brood may comprise about 100 young.

Another *Procambarus* was found by A. Nolte in the Mississippi drainage near Starkville, and is thus here termed *Procambarus* sp. "Starkville". It is sand-coloured with irregular dark grey spots all over its body, including the legs and claws. The spots sometimes merge together and are large on the carapace and the relatively broad claws, but comparatively small on the abdomen and telson. The tips of the claws are red.

stone terrain and in natural springs and sink-holes. This explains why its eyes are exceptionally small, although it has supposedly been demonstrated that the species is not light-sensitive. It thrives at temperatures between 20

The ground colour of another species, here called *Procambarus* sp. "Louisiana" (in reference

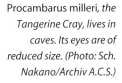

North world crayfishes
Large American species

Left: Female of the Marble Cray with eggs…

…and with hatched larvae between its pleopods (right).

If Marble Crays are kept in soft water, they will turn beautifully blue within a few weeks.

to its provenance) is a grey- brown. The edges of the head and thorax are marked with dark brown, and a broad dark band runs from behind the eye along the middle of the carapace to the abdomen, where it continues between the vertical stripes which delimit the segments of the abdomen and meet at their lower ends in a wedge shape, creating an overall zigzag pattern. A brown band also runs along the middle of the telson, and the upper surfaces of the head, tail fan, and claws are sprinkled with fine brown dots.

.

Neither the origin nor the identity of the often-maintained Marble Cray is clear, but it is thought to be an American species, and because it has an annulus ventralis, it must be a Cambarid, possibly even a *Procambarus*. Its basic coloration is brownish, but if it is kept in soft water for a few weeks or so it can change to a beautiful blue! The species grows to about 7 centimetres and is said to be rather aggressive. In addition, it eats plants or chops them off.

As a rule, New World crayfishes are determined by means of the first pleopods in males, transformed into gonopods, or by the hooks on their walking legs. Unfortunately neither of these features is of any help with regard to the Marble Cray - all individuals look like females. Nevertheless they reproduce without problem and very prolifically. At a carapace length of 3.5 to 4 centimetres upwards, they start laying eggs which they carry about as thick packets attached to the abdomen. Large females can lay up to 200 eggs! During development, bluish-white spots appear on these eggs. At 27°C, the larvae hatch after about 12 days and during the final stage of their development they exhibit a blackish-brown, V-shaped pattern on their carapaces. Six or seven days after hatching, the young climb

down from their mother and become independent. The probable explanation for this reproductive phenomenon is parthenogenesis. In such cases there are as a rule only females, though exceptionally males may occur as well. Reproduction is made possible by the fusion of two (haploid or diploid) egg cells within the same individual. It has also occasionally been suggested that these crays may be hermaphroditic – i.e. that they possess the gonads of both sexes – against this is the fact that copulation has never been observed. But hermaphroditic crays do in fact exist. They have been known for a long time from the south of South America and belong to the Parastacidae (southern hemisphere crays), specifically the genera *Samastacus*, *Virilastacus*, and *Parastacus*. Some of the species concerned live in caves. Adult individuals that take the role of females develop a broader abdomen.

North world crayfishes
Cambarellus species

This male of Procambarus alleni is one of the neon-blue indidviduals.

Procambarus leonensis - here a female - doesn't feel well if you keep it too warm for al longer period.

American *Cambarellus* species

The smallest American crayfishes, called "dwarf river crays" in the aquarium literature, belong to the small subfamily known as the Cambarellinae. The name of their genus, *Cambarellus*, is the diminutive of *Cambarus* and means "little *Cambarus*", alluding to the size of its representatives.

These crayfishes are said to attain only two to four centimetres or a little more, and are to be found from Mexico along the Gulf Coast to northern of Florida. There are thus some species that can tolerate lower temperatures. They can be kept and bred in small aquaria, are hardy, and reach sexual maturity at the age of about three months. Egg numbers vary from 5 to 70 depending on the species and the size and condition of the female.

Cambarellus shuffeldtii is a tiny species that grows to only two or three centimetres. If it is kept in a very small tank, it is essential to ensure that the small amount of water is kept as free of nitrate as possible. These crays have no special requirements, but females often remain hidden during the daytime – in general you will see only the bolder males.

At night (or during the twilight periods) both sexes (which can be determined as in *Procambarus* species) seem to be more active. They are not aggressive towards their own kind, and are found at rather high population densities in nature. In the aquarium too they can be kept in a group of several conspecifics, as cannibalism is comparatively rare. Two forms of this species are known, one with four stripes and another with an irregular pattern of spots. In the wild, both forms can be found syntopic (in the same place). Intermediate forms are unknown, even though striped parents may, for example, produce spotted babies.

Cambarellus are believed to be descended from northern ancestors which spread further south. Today, however, in Mexico *Cambarellus* are distributed only between the 8th and 22nd parallels of latitude. The species involved are *Cambarellus montezumae* and its subspecies - which some authors now regard as valid species - and closely allied forms such as *C. alvarezi* and *C. chapalanus*.

Cambarellus montezumae was originally described as a *Cambarus*. The specific name honours Moctzezuma (Montezuma) II. This

North world crayfishes
Cambarellus species

Aztec ruler, who was killed in 1520, lived in Tenochtitlán, which once stood where Mexico City stands today. And because this little cray is to be found around Mexico City, , it has carried Montezuma's name since 1857. Its subspecies are distributed further east and southeast. Because they differ from each other only in small details, it is difficult to distinguish them, at least in live specimens.

Cambarellus chapalanus is yellowish or brownish, with two dark double bands (not necessarily always clearly visible) running along the sides of the cephalothorax and abdomen. These crays can be kept even in a decoratively planted aquarium: *Cambarellus* neither eat plants nor do they chop them off. But they do use them a lot to leave the bottom, climbing about on their leaves and stalks. They are very active in contrast to their larger relatives, which in general move rather sedately and spend a lot of time in their hiding-places. They seem to be neither crepuscular nor sedentary, and are visible throughout the day.

Females are a little larger than males and their abdomens are broader, while the smooth claws are longer in males. The annulus ventralis of the females takes the form of an inverted U. Females lay between 30 and 40 eggs, about 1.5 mm in diameter, which under favourable circumstances develop within two weeks. A uniformly high temperature (around 25°C), clean water, and strong aeration will encourage rapid development, without losses.

A very similar species, which may be coloured brownish or bright orange, has appeared in the aquarium literature variously as *C. patzcuarensis* and *C. zempoalensis*. The former would mean that these crays originate from Michoacán, the latter from Morelos - both states in the Mexican Republic. Either way, this Orange Crayfish has similar requirements to *Cambarellus montezumae* and other Mexican species and can be kept and bred in the same way.

The males of Cherax quadricarinatus *can be recognized easily because they have crescent-shaped red spots on their claws.*

Below: This female of Cherax quadricarinatus *carries eggs.*

Right: Recently hatched young crayfishes on the abdomen of a Cherax quadricarinatus-*female;*

Left: Cherax quadricarinatus-*baby with its yolk on its back;*

South world crayfishes
Australian *Cherax* species

Cherax species

The rivers, lakes, and swamps of Australia, New Zealand, and New Guinea are home to some 110 different endemic crayfish species, which have been assigned to various genera. *Cherax*, *Engaeus*, and *Euastacus* are the largest, each comprising some 30, 40 or more species, while the numbers in *Astacopsis*, *Engaewa*, *Geocharax*, *Gramastacus*, *Paranephrops*, *Parastacoides*, and *Tenuibranchiurus* are considerably smaller.

Many of these crays inhabit clearly defined ranges, which are often rather small. According to their type and provenance, they are called by a number of different names,. There are crawchies (= small crayfishes), jilgies (*C. quinquecarinatus*; *C. crassimanus*), koonacs (*C. plebejus*; *C. glaber*), lobbies (= lobsters), marrons (*C. tenuimanus*), and yabbies (*C. destructor*; *C. albidus*). Some of them are real giants, and they even include the biggest crayfish in the world. This species grows to a body length of 60 centimetres and a weight of four kilos. But there are small species, too, which attain only about 20 millimetres and which are - at least in some cases – exceptionally attractively coloured, so we can hope for further interesting imports.

Up to now, only *Cherax* species have been imported, with *Cherax destructor*, the popular Yabby, the best known. Although wild crayfishes are protected in Australia, they are bred on special farms for the delicatessen trade and for export. The Yabby is a very colourful species that can be heartily recommended, even though its specific name means "destroyer". It grows to about 20 centimetres and has broad, powerful claws in both sexes. It is appreciably less aggressive towards conspecific than is *Procambarus clarkii*, and rarely hunts for fishes: these slow-moving crayfishes seem unable to catch fast-moving prey items. But on the other hand they are persistent diggers, such that any rocks must be positioned with great care, directly on the (glass) bottom of the aquarium.

Cherax destructor is a very successful and adaptable crayfish that has conquered large parts of eastern Australia as its natural habitat and which particularly common. It lives in the cool wet regions of Victoria, in the southern

Cherax-*males lack the conspicious gonopods which make sex discrimination in American crayfishes so easy.*

In Cherax-*females, the genital openings can be easily seen on the base of third pair of walking-legs.*

coastal areas, and in the snow-covered mountains and also in the hot and arid areas of central Australia. It is said to bury itself in the mud in dry years, in order to survive until the next rains. These crayfishes are said to be most abundant in the western districts of Buronga, Menindee, Balranald, Bourke, and Condobolin.

Photos of *Cherax destructor* almost always show a brilliant sky-blue cray with red joints to its chelipeds. But not all Yabbies are coloured like this: - there are also whitish-blue individuals others which are dark blue, and yet others that are almost brown on the back and abdomen; their claws are dark blue with heavy patterning on the upper part. And their coloration may also change when they moult.

As imported crayfish suffer during the long transit from their native land, unfortunately most specimens offered for sale are in generally bad condition, and quite often have legs, claws, or antennae missing. These will, of course, be replaced at the next moult, but first they must survive the move to a new home and settle in. Provided all goes well at this

South world crayfishes
Australian *Cherax* species

Right: Most Cherax destructor *are bright blue.*

Left: These black crays with the bright red antennas belong to the species Cherax preissii. *They need cool, oxygen-rich water. (Photo: F. Teigler/Archiv A.C.S.)*

Cherax tenuimanus *can be ochre-coloured or reddish-brown. But there are also blue, brownish-violet and black individuals of* Cherax tenuimanus.

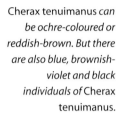

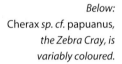

Below: Cherax *sp. cf.* papuanus, *the Zebra Cray, is variably coloured.*

South world crayfishes
Australian *Cherax* species

stage, they will subsequently prove be easy to keep. It is sometimes recommended that a little salt should be added to the aquarium water, but this is not actually necessary. These crays are sensitive to fertilisers containing iron and medications that contain copper. Fungal diseases can supposedly be avoided by feeding with dry oak leaves.

Cherax quadricarinatus lives on the northeast coast of Australia in eastern Arnhemland, a region whose rivers drain into the Van Diemen Gulf and thus the Timor Sea, and also into rivers further east that flow into the Gulf of Carpentaria. Except for a small area in the east, the entire Cape York peninsula is also included in its natural distribution. In addition, it has been released in recent years into waters in southern Queensland and north-eastern New South Wales. The species is more slender than *C. destructor* and has appreciably longer and narrower claws. In addition it has two or three pairs of spines on the rostrum, absent from *C. destructor*. Meanwhile *C. destructor* has a kind of "keel" between the third and fourth pairs of legs, lacking in *C. quadricarinatus*.

The basic bluish colour of the latter may vary from blue-green to brown, but may also be a brilliant light blue in places. The back and tail are flecked with yellow or brown, above all in females. In males, the outer edge of each claw has a striking, elongated, brilliant red blotch, which is the reason why the Australians call it the Red Claw. This species also grows to about 20 centimetres, but is not very aggressive towards conspecifics. It can also be kept in the same tank as fishes - provided the latter are not too small.

These two *Cherax* species are not at all demanding, but do need to be kept warm, at about 25 to 28°C. At such temperatures they grow exceptionally rapidly and will reach sexual maturity as early as their fourth month. It should be noted that male *Cherax* lack the stirrup-like gonopods that make sex determination in *Procambarus* species so easy, but if you look at them from below, you will see the genital openings at the base of the fourth (last) pair of walking legs. Normally there are two such openings, one on each side, and they are considerably smaller than in females, in which they are found at the base of the

second pair of legs. It should be added that there are specimens with both male and female genital openings! But as the latter are without function, all these crays are all just males.

These *Cherax* species can also be bred easily under aquarium conditions. Copulation follows a similar procedure to that in *P. clarkii*. The male throws the female onto her back and attaches packets of sperm between her posterior legs. Some hours later, she lays about 100 to 300 dark grey eggs, the diameter of which is about two millimetres. The eggs gradually swell and become lighter in colour, so that you can see the development inside. At 25°C it takes about 21 days before the young finally hatch. The tiny crayfishes readily accept any kind of food, but unfortunately this includes each other! If the prevailing conditions (water quality, aeration, temperature, food) are favourable, the young can grow to about eight or nine centimetres total length within nine months.

Cherax preissii is often black, but also sometimes black-brown or brown-green with red antennae. It can be recognised by its four head ridges, including that on the rostrum. The rostrum has no or only weakly developed spines, and the carapace is smooth without any button-like protruberances. The claws are broad and compressed, and the legs and arms are hairless on their inner sides. These crays are imported as "*C. plebejus*". *C. preissii* attains a total length of about 20 cm and is said to dig enthusiastically in the wild. This "koonak" is found in the vicinity of Perth and south to Albany, and is more common inland and in the mountains, preferring cool, oxygen-rich water. It survives periods of drought by burying itself deep.

Another *Cherax* species has been available since 2000, usually labelled as *Cherax misolicus*. It is, however, doubtful whether it is in fact that New Guinea species. It seems more likely that it is a local form or colour variety of *Cherax papuanus*, a species native to Lake Marguerite (also known as Lake Kutubu) which lies at 850 m above sea level in Papua and is connected by the rivers Samaka and Mobi with the Kikori, a river that empties into the Gulf of Papua.

South world crayfishes
Australian *Cherax* species

The type specimens used for the description of this species measured 90 and 84 mm body length, but it seems to grow at least a little larger. The sexes can in this case also be determined by the size of the claws; which are particularly broad and powerful in males. Until the identity of this cray has become clear, we should - as many aquarists already do – follow the lead of C. Lukhaup and use the popular name Zebra Cray, which very aptly describes the light-coloured banding on the abdomen. This species tolerates pH values between 7 and 8, and does well in water that is reasonably warm (between 21 and 25°C). It feeds eagerly on twigs and dead leaves, which should be offered as well as food tablets and frozen (fish-) foods.

Cherax tenuimanus is an Australian species that is also occasionally imported. Its scientific specific name is derived from the Latin words *tenuis* meaning thin, and *manus* meaning hand, referring to its slender claws. These crayfishes do indeed have much narrower claws than, for example, the Yabby and the not yet imported *Euastacus* species, but they are not much smaller than those of *Cherax quadricarinatus*.

The Australian popular name for this cray is Marron, which means "the maroon one". It is easily recognisable by several characteristics: firstly, it has five longitudinal ridges on the upper surface of its head, secondly there are three pairs of short spines on the rostrum, and thirdly there are two small spines on the middle of the tail fan. In addition the armour is not smooth in these crays, but covered with small lateral "knobs" on its sides, and the claws are especially slender (as already mentioned) and never covered in cushions of fine hair

This species can be of quite variable in colour: most individuals are brownish, but they can also tend to dark violet or black, and there are even reddish-brown, brilliant sky blue, or dark blue individuals. The Marron is said to be the largest known *Cherax* species; it grows up to 38.5 centimetres total length. But individuals with a carapace length of only 7 to 8 centimetres are termed adult.

Cherax tenuimanus lives in southwestern Australia. Its natural range originally comprised only river drainages from the Murray to the Kent, extending from Perth over Harvey and Pemberton to Albany. But today these crays can be found in the coastal regions further to the north and to the east, and even further inland. They have been in part been deliberately introduced by Man, and they have sometimes spread via irrigation channels, and in yet other cases they are kept in large breeding ponds from which escapes into natural waters regularly occur. Both introduction into new regions and cultivation in ponds have had rather limited success - the species prospers only in waters that are richly oxygenated.

For this reason the species isn't be found in every billabong (water hole), but lives in the deep running water of larger rivers. It is found primarily over sandy bottoms and in places where detritus has accumulated. In contrast to other *Cherax* species it does not dig deep burrows but during the day remains in the shelter of stones and accumulations of dead wood, largely to avoid falling prey to cormorants. Of course they do enlarge their retreats when necessary, shovelling out sand and gravel. At sunset they leave their hiding-places and search for food. Their population density seems to depend on the availability of hiding-places.

These crays are rather aggressive among themselves, so their aquarium should be as spacious as possible. They can, of course, also be raised in separate tanks and put together when they are sexually mature. Even more important, however, are good aeration and efficient filtration that ensures constant good water quality. In addition the Marron tolerates only temperatures of 15 to 20°C , the optimum being 17°C. Adult specimens may tolerate 25°C for a short period of time, but young ones will die in such warm water. The pH should be in the range 7.0 to 8.0

Right: This still undetermined species of Cherax has been imported from New Guinea quite recently. It can be coloured bright orange, grey or blue.

Upper left: This land crab (Cardisoma armatum) lives in West-Africa.

Upper right: Land-crabs build deep, tube-like holes in the sand.

Middle left: Tha Asian river crab Demanietta sirikit is even brighter coloured in nature.

Middle right: Fiddler-Crab of the genus Uca.

Below: The most often imported crab of the family Grapsidae is Pseudosesarma moeshi, here a male.

Crabs

In the suborder Brachyura, the true crabs, which without doubt represent the most highly developed crustaceans of all, we find a large number of marine species, but also a few that are to a greater or lesser extent adapted to brackish or fresh water. Of these, the most interesting for the freshwater aquarist are a number of members of the families Potamonidae, Grapsidae, Ocypodidae, and Gecarcinidae.

Potamoidea (river crabs)

The river crabs - it would be too imprecise taxonomically to call them freshwater crabs - of the super-family Potamoidea are the only large group of crabs that comprises only freshwater forms which spend their entire life cycle in fresh water. That is to say, they do not migrate back into brackish or sea water to deposit their brood. There is a wide range of forms, from strictly fluviatile crabs to amphibious species and true land crabs which have left the water completely. They are found in dry forests and tropical lakes and rice fields, and some species spend the summer "baked" into the ground part of the time. Unfortunately, they are seldom found in pet-shops, which may be due to the fact that they do not live in colonies, but solitarily, so that they cannot be caught in large numbers. They live not only in the tropics, but also in the countries of the northern Mediterranean. Most are well camouflaged, as many of their enemies,

Below: Rver crab from Panama.
(Photo: M. Keijman)

e.g. birds and mammals, attack from above. There are, however, a number of colourful species in Southeast Asia, for example the members of the genus *Phricothelphusa* and the land-dwelling species *Demanietta sirikit*.

If these crabs are attacked under water, they fight vigorously and nip! The aquarist who wants to keep them should prepare a shallow aquarium with a large bottom area, and provide them with the opportunity to climb up above the water level. As their excreta can lead to self-poisoning, the water must be filtered biologically and changed regularly. Single individuals can be kept in smaller tanks, but if you want to keep a number of specimens, these aggressive crabs must be able to avoid one other and to find shelter in caves that are not too close together. Shelter can be provided by stones and wood (which the crabs will nibble), and twigs complete with dead leaves. It is, unfortunately, not possible to plant such an aquarium, as the crabs will eat anything green or chop it off. Besides, they dig a lot.

But river crabs, which in the wild eat algae, mosses, leaves, and higher plants) are not only vegetarian, even though they readily eat lettuce, spinach, pieces of apple, food tablets, frozen Brussels sprouts, or boiled peas when kept in aquaria. They also hunt for insects and their larvae, snails, earthworms, frogs, and fishes. So you can also give them meat (chopped beef heart, fish, or mussel), shrimp, *Mysis*, *Artemia*, bloodworm, and live *Tubifex*, whiteworm, and

Crabs
Brachyura

mealworms - in short, any kind of food that you would give to larger aquarium fishes.

It is also necessary to cover the aqua-terrarium tightly because these crabs are skilful climbers and will use the smallest gap to escape, or even lift loosely fitted covers, perhaps even heavy lids or glass panes, in order to get out. If they do escape, you should try to find them as quickly as possible - otherwise they will dry out. For this purpose, you can put a wet sponge on the floor and rely on the ability of these crabs to detect any kind of moisture without difficulty. In most cases you will find them underneath the sponge the next morning.

Grapsidae (mangrove crabs)

The so-called mangrove crabs of the genus *Sesarma* are imported from time to time; they belong to the family Grapsidae (jumping-crabs). Where they occur in the wild, they are found in large numbers and can be caught in large quantities. They are able to jump as much as five to ten times their own body width, and they usually live in rocky habitats in coastal regions. They have conquered the entire tropics and subtropical regions, where they live in the tidal zones of the seashore, the brackish river estuaries, and mangrove swamps. They are apparently currently moving into fresh water too. Some of them are extremely adept at climbing: *Metopaulias depressus* lives almost exclusively on tree roots and uses the water that collects in the "cups" of bromeliads for breeding! *Nepentes* crabs live on trees that are heavily covered with epiphytes and likewise utilise the water collected by the plants.

The Red Mangrove Crab is one of about 150 species which resemble each other very closely. They all remain small, their shell barely exceeding four centimetres in diameter. The species most frequently offered for sale has hitherto been labelled *Sesarma bidens*, but the latest wisdom is that it is actually *Pseudosesarma moeshi*. The natural range of this group is said to include Japan, Hongkong, the Philippines, Sulawesi, the Nicobars, the Andaman Islands, and Sri Lanka (Ceylon).

With a very few exceptions, mangrove crabs do not actually live in fresh water, although in the wild they do migrate via brackish water to fresh, so that adults do not generally come to any ham

The fiddler fdrab Uca pugnax *is imported from Ecuador. It is a rather hardy species.*
(Photo: F. Schäfer)

if kept in freshwater aquaria . If you want to do keep them healthy, just add some common salt (sodium chloride) to the water, change a percentage of the water regularly, and provide an adequate oxygen supply via aeration or filtration. As they lead an amphibious life, the aquarium should be only half filled, and roots and stones should be arranged so as to not only create numerous hiding-places, but also provide spacious "perches" out of the water. It is also important that their home is tightly-covered so that they cannot escape and the air space remains warm (to avoid chilling) and humid. Ideally the water should be heated to 24 -25°C and circulated using a small filter or aeration. At the same time the lighting will ensure an air temperature of 28 - 30°C and the necessary high degree of humidity (more than 80%).

The sexes are easy to determine in all crabs, because the forward-folded pleon is narrower in the male than in the female, and his claws are sometimes larger. But unfortunately we cannot hope to breed mangrove crabs in captivity, as at spawning time the female must seek out brackish or sea water. The 3000 or so eggs are carried around by the female, attached to the underside of her pleon, until they hatch, and need to be kept moist. After six to eight weeks the so-called zoea-larvae are released into the open water. Rearing them has proved extremely difficult under aquarium conditions.

Ocypodidae (fiddler crabs)

From time to time crabs of the family Ocypodidae are imported as well. Of these, the so-called running-crabs of the genus *Octypode* are unsuitable for aquarium maintenance. They are fast-running crabs that populate the dry higher parts of sandy tropical beaches, away from the water. They are thus in no way aquatic and certainly not freshwater denizens - they even need absolutely clean sea water to drink.

The fiddler crabs also belong to this family, and

Crabs
Brachyura

River crab from the rio Xingu in Brazil.

they too live on tropical beaches, but occupying mudflats that remain constantly moist. They need mud to survive, retreating into their burrows when the tide comes in and closing the entrance from inside. Only a few occur in brackish water, and even fewer in fresh. Most crabs of this group offered for sale belong to the genus *Uca*. Their German popular name of *Winkerkrabbe*, which means waving crab, alludes to the fact that the males develop a single oversized claw - the weight of which may be half that of the entire animal - and which in most cases is also strikingly coloured. To try and attract a female, the male raises and waves this huge claw, while the other, which is of normal size, is used for eating. Females have do not have an enlarged claw. The gestures of the males vary from species to species, but all look like waving. In England and France these crabs are called fiddler crabs and *crabes-violonistes* respectively, because the large claws make these little chaps look as if they are carrying a fiddle (violin) around with them!

Once a male has successfully courted a female, mating occurs belly to belly. The copulation may take only a few minutes, but equally more than half an hour. Both partners tenderly hold and touch each other, as if in a warm embrace. At the same time, the male repeatedly knocks on the back of the female, using his enlarged claw. Although the females will lay eggs in captivity, carry them about, and finally wash them off into the water with vigorous beats of the tail, successful breeding under aquarium conditions doesn't seem a likely prospect. The larvae are really tiny and in nature lead a pelagic life, metamorphosing through a number of stages and feeding on particular types of plankton.

Hence rearing them would be virtually impossible.

Gercarcinidae (land crabs)

Land crabs of the family Gecarcinidae have also repeatedly been imported. Some of them grow to a respectable size, their shells measuring around 20 centimetres across! They include the American *Gecarcinus* and the Indo-Pacific *Gecarcoidea*. Both are totally unsuitable for freshwater aquaria. They are exclusively land-living and populate the upper, dry parts of sand and coral beaches. Adult individuals are the best-adapted of all crabs for life on land, breathing almost exclusively via lungs and drowning in water. In the wild they find shelter in fissures in rocks and shallow cavities beneath stones and tree roots, where it is cool and dry. Their water requirement is supplied by eating plants, and they also collect dew at night on their hairy legs! And they are generally more active in the cool of the night than during the daytime.

By contrast, species of the genus *Cardisoma* are suitable for maintenance in an aqua-terrarium. In the wild they live in salt marshes, in burrows that they dig themselves. These are sometimes more than a metre deep and always contain the water essential to these crabs, which breathe via gills.

Even though adult crabs of both groups live on land, their eggs develop only in the sea. After copulation, the females lay fertilised eggs and carry them about, attached to their hairy pleo-pods. During their development, the eggs change colour from orange or red to a greyish-green. Eventually the females make their way to the sea, often in large groups. This often takes place at full moon, as the timing of the whole procedure is determined by the phases of the moon. Aided by vigorous movements of the abdomen, they rinse their eggs off into the surf – a hazardous process, at least for *Gecarcinus* and *Gecarcoidea*, whose gills are so atrophied that they are at risk of drowning. When the larvae hatch, they start a planktonic life. During their time at sea they develop through a number of stages, some of them reminiscent of shrimps, until finally they leave the water as fully-formed crabs.

An aqua-terrarium for a group of *Cardisoma* should be fairly spacious (150 x 70 cm) and not too shallow as a deep layer of sand is required so

Crabs
Brachyura

River crabs (this is the Indian species Sartoriana spinigera) *eat and/or destroy plants in the tank.*

that the crabs can construct their burrows. You can, of course, use stones and roots to provide additional cavities, but such decor must be well-founded. Part of the sandy area of the aqua-terrarium should be kept covered with fresh leaves (preferably of those of fruit trees) or lettuce. The crabs will feed on them and deposit their excrement on them, so that it is easier to keep the substrate clean.

The small water reservoir (at most a quarter of the available space) should be just deep enough for the crabs to be able to breathe without difficulty while resting on the bottom. You will then see how the used water is expelled via the mouth. At the same time, the crabs should be able to raise their respiratory openings (which are located at the insertions of the walking-legs) above the water level. The lower layers of sand of the land area of your terrarium must be kept moist or wet, and because of the high metabolic rate of the crabs, the water must be changed very often. It should be brackish, and this is best achieved using some sea salt.

It is also important to cover the aqua-terrarium well. Neither the crabs nor the warm, moist air (28–30°C, humidity 80%+) should be able to escape! If the air space is too cool then the crabs will seek out a spot in under the warm light to avoid becoming chilled.

Because of their aggression, the crab community should consist of individuals matched as closely as possible in size and strength, so that none is easy prey for the rest. Newly-moulted specimens must be able to find shelter or else be separated from the rest.

All species are very good climbers and escape easily.

This is Parathelphusula *sp., a river crab from Bengal.*

These crabs, too, eat almost anything, so you can give them the same food as the river crabs. However, the bulk of their diet should consist of vegetables and fruit, not least because all crabs are sensitive to the breakdown products of animal material, which may cause (auto-)toxicity. Their tolerance of such waste products will generally be greater if the water is mineral-rich or contains salt.

Most land crabs can live for more than ten years and become hand tame.

Literature tips

KRUSTER ALLGEMEIN:

ALTEVOGT, R. (1971): Unterklasse Höhere Krebse. In: Grzimeks Tierleben 1: Niedere Tiere, Kap. 16: Die Krebstiere. Zürich: 468–506.
Arbeitsgemeinschaft Wirbellose im Internet: www.wirbellose.de
RENNER, M. (1967): Leitfaden für das Zoologische Praktikum, Stuttgart: 223–244;
WERNER, U. (1993): Ausgefallene Aquarienpfleglinge, Landbuch-Verlag Hannover, 191 S.

GARNELEN:

BITTER, F. (2000): Fächergarnelen. Aquaristik aktuell 3-4: 74-78.
CAI , Y. & N. K. NG (1999): A revision of the Caridina serrata species group, with descriptions of five new species (Crustacea: Decapoda: Caridea: Atyidae). Journ. Nat. Hist., 33: 1603-1638.
CHACE, F. A. Jr. (1983): The Atya-like shrimps of the Indo-Pacific Region (Decapoda: Atyidae). Smithsonian Contributions to Zoology 384.
GÖTHEL, H. (1986): Zwei Süßwassergarnelen für das Gesellschaftsbecken. DATZ 39: 67–69.
GORTZYTZA, H. (1990): Die Zucht von Süßwassergarnelen – eine Herausforderung? DATZ 43: 599–601.
HANSON, J. A. & H. L. GODWIN (1977): Shrimp and prawn farming in the western hemisphere. Dowden, Hutchinson & Ross, Inc., Pennsylvania: 193 ff.
LEIENDECKER, E. & U. (1982): An ihren Scheren kann man sie erkennen: Süßwassergarnelen. Aquarien-Magazin, Heft 3: 167–172.
LING, Shao-Wen (1977): Aquaculture in Southeast Asia. Wash. Sea Grant Publ., Seattle & London: 94-101.
KURIAN, C. V. & V. O. SEBASTIAN (1982): Prawns and prawn fisheries of India. Hindustan Publ. Corp. (India), Delhi-110007: 62 ff.
MORI, F. (1998): Asiatische Süßwassergarnelen. Aquaristik aktuell 7-8: 6-11.
Ng, P. K. L. & D. G. B. CHIA (1994): Die Riesenbachgarnele. DATZ 47: 644–648.
ROCHARD, Chr. & E. (1984): Contribution à la maintenance et la reproduction de la crevette d'eau douce Macrobrachium lanchesteri. AQUARAMA, Heft 79, 21 ff.
SUBRAHMANYAM, M. (…) : Studies on growth of the giant freshwater prawn Macrobrachium rosenbergii (De Man). Prawn Breeding Unit CIFA, Andhra Pradesh, India: 340-351.
WERNER, U. (1987): Mehr als nur kulinarische Köstlichkeit – Süßwassergarnelen der Gattung Macrobrachium Bate, 1868. TI 84: 37–39.
WERNER, U. (1987): Eine Garnele mit 'Fächerhänden': Atya moluccensis. DATZ 40: 283–284.
WERNER, U. (1997): Die Blaue Fächergarnele. Eine neu eingeführte Atya-Art aus Westafrika. Das Aquarium 337: 12–15.
WERNER, U. (1999): Neue Garnelen für das Süßwasseraquarium. Das Aquarium 363: 22-28.
WERNER, U. (2001): Die Maya-Garnele aus Palenque. TI 159: 47-48.

KREBSE:

ARNOLD, A. (1989): Nochmals zum Kuba-Süßwasserkrebs, Procambarus cubensis. AT 36: 24–26.
BERGER, M. (1985): Cuba-Süßwasserkrebs. AT 32: 153.
BOETGER, C. (1949): Das Auftreten des Amerikanischen Flußkrebses in Niedersachsen. Natur und Volk (5/6): 143–146.
BOTT, R. (1949): Amerikanische Flußkrebse im Main. Natur und Volk (6/6): 139–143.
CARROLL, P. N. (Ed.) (1980): A Yabbie Pot Pourri. Vorlesungstexte u. a. d. Hawesbury Agric. Coll. u. d. Univ. New England, Armidale.
CONVERT, C. (1982): Reproduction de Procambarus clarkii. AQUARAMA 64, 14 ff.
DOST, U. (1995): Flußkrebse im Aquarium. DATZ 48: 502–508.
Fisheries Department Perth (1985): Marron and Marron farming. Ext. Publ. Sect. Fish. Dept. Perth, WA: 39 pp.
Fisheries of Western Australia, Homepage: http://www.wa.gov.au/westfish/aqua/broc/idfresh/idfresh02.html

GRABOWSKI, T. (1998): Über Krebse. Thannhausen/Mindelzell; 47 S.
GRÜNWALD, H. (1970): Einwanderer aus Amerika. Amerikanische Flußkrebse im Lippe-Seiten-Kanal. Heimatkalender des Kreises Dinslaken (NRW).
HENDRIX, A. N. & W. F. LOFTUS (2000): Distribution and relative abundance of the crayfishes Procambarus alleni (Faxon) and P. fallax (Hagen) in southern Florida. Wetlands 20, 1: 194-199.
HOBBS, H. H. Jr. (1972): Crayfishes (Astacidae) of north and middle America. Biota of Freshwater Ecosystems 9: 173 pp.
HOLTHUIS, L. B. (1949): Decapoda macrura. With a revision of the New Guinea Parastacidae. Zool. Res. Dutch New Guinea Exp. 1939, 3: 37-329 + Plates. In: Nova Guinea, Ne Series V. Leiden.
JORDAN, F. , J. B. KIMBERLY, C. C. McIVOR & S. J. MILLER (1996): Spatial ecology of the crayfish Procambarus alleni in a Florida wetland mosaic. 21 pp.
LECHLEITER, S. (1995): Flußkrebse im Aquarium. DATZ 48: 745.
LEHMANN, H. (1986): Erfahrungen mit Kuba-Süßwasserkrebsen. AT 33: 102.
LIETSCH, P. (1984): Zur Pflege und Zucht des südamerikanischen Sumpfkrebses (Procambarus troglodytes). AT 31: 313.
LUKHAUP, Ch. (2000): Florida-Lobster, Blickfang im Süßwasseraquarium. Aquaristik aktuell 8: 32-36.
LUKHAUP, Ch. (2001): Procambarus milleri, der Mandarinenkrebs. Aquaristik aktuell 3-4: 70-73.
MANCINI, A. (1989): Les Ecrevisses (Crustacea: Decapoda: Astacoidea, Parastacoidea) dans l'aquarium. Revue fr. Aquariol., 16 (1), 7:11–21.
MERRICK, J. R. & C. N. Lambert (1991): The Yabby, Marron and Red Claw. Production and marketing. Nat. Lib. Austr., 175 pp.
MÜLLER, H. (1973): Die Flußkrebse. Die langschwänzigen Decapoda Mitteleuropas und ihre wirtschaftliche Bedeutung. Brehm-Bücherei Nr. 121, Wittenberg-Lutherstadt, 2. bearb. Aufl..
NOLTE, A. (1996): Der Zwergflußkrebs Cambarellus shuffeldtii. DATZ 49: 567–569.
OTT, G. (1990): Flußkrebse. Der Amerikanische Flußkrebs, Orconectes limosus, ist meist nur aus dem Kochtopf bekannt. Das Aquarium, Heft 8: 5–10.
RASCH, P. (1985): Ritter ohne Furcht und Tadel. Pflege und Zucht des Amerikanischen Teichkrebses. Aquarien-Magazin 10: 428–433.
ROUSE, D. B & I. Kartamulia (1992): Influence of salinity and temperature on molting and survival of the Australian freshwater crayfish (Cherax tenuimanus). Aquaculture 105: 47-52.
SCHLÜTER, M. (1989): Flußkrebse aus Australien. Ritter in farbenfroher Rüstung. DATZ 42: 526–528.
WERNER, U. (1987): Gaumenfreude-Augenweide: Procambarus clarkii, der Nordamerikanische Teichkrebs. DATZ 40: 529–531.
SCHMIDT-HERZER, K. (1999): Die Krebspest - eine unendliche Geschichte? Das Aquarium 361: 3-9.
WERNER, U. (1999): Biologie und Pflege von Cherax-Arten (Parastacidae, Crustacea) im Aquarium. In: Riehl, R. & H. Greven (Hersg.): Fortpflanzungsbiologie der Aquarienfische. Symposiumsband. Bornheim: 240 S.
WERNER, U. (2001): Zwergkrebse. Die Arten der Gattung Cambarellus sind in Mexiko heimisch. Das Aquarium 383: 16-19.
WERNER, U. (2001): Der "Marron", Cherax tenuimanus, ein australischer Krebs, neu für das Süßwasseraquarium eingeführt. Das Aquarium 386: 8-12.

KRABBEN:

CHIA, D. G. B. & P. K. L. Ng (1994): Die Riesenlandkrabben von Malaysia. DATZ 47: 30–34.
ESTERBAUER, H. (1983): Notizen zur Biologie und Pflege der Süßwasserkrabbe Potamon potamios. Das Aquarium 27, Heft 293 (11): 11–14.
KADEN, J. (1991): Strandläufer. DATZ 44: 22–27.
KUPFERER, R. (1991): Mangrovekrabben (mit einer Anmerkung von D. Schaller). DATZ 44: 492–493.
MANCINI, A. (1995): Crabes et pagures d'eau douce, d'eau saumâtre et...de terre. AQUARAMA 142: 16–22.
VON HAGEN, H.-O. (1983): Vom Strand auf den Markt. Südamerikas Landkrebse leben gefährlich. Das TIER: 72–75.

Index of species illustrated

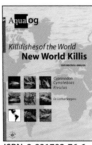

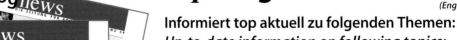
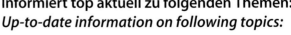